*Cinetek* series

Sunless

o

Sans soleil

*Jon Kear*

FLICKS
BOOKS

A CIP catalogue record for this book is available from the British Library.

ISBN 0 948911 37 9

First published in 1999 by

Flicks Books
29 Bradford Road
Trowbridge
Wiltshire  BA14 9AN
England
*tel*   +44 1225 767728
*fax*  +44 1225 760418

Printed and bound in Great Britain by Antony Rowe Ltd.

Dedicated to the memory of Sanxo de Monamór

# Contents

He liked the fragility of those moments suspended in time, those memories whose only function had been to leave behind nothing but memories. (From the soundtrack of *Sunless*)

\*   \*   \*

An unknown woman reads and comments on letters she has received from a friend – a freelance cameraman who travels around the world and is particularly attached to those two 'extreme poles of survival', Japan and Africa. The cameraman questions himself on the meaning of this representation of the world of which he is perpetually the instrument, and the role of these memories which he helps to form. One of his Japanese colleagues responds in his own way by attacking the images stored in memory, taking them apart on the synthesiser. A cinema producer takes advantage of this situation and makes a film out of it, but rather than casting these people as themselves and showing their relationships, both real and supposed, prefers to serve up parts of the material in the form of a musical composition. From these memories, placed side by side, is born a fictive memory... (Chris. Marker)[1]

This is how Chris. Marker has described the basic plot of *Sunless*, a deceptively simple description of the film's extraordinary journey through time, place and memory. Ostensibly an essay and a travelogue in which an unnamed cameraman returns to Japan, the film is an attempt to come to terms with the continuities and changes that have occurred within this country in the aftermath of the Second World War. As we follow the cameraman's travels across the country, we become aware that, for the cameraman, the places we visit are permeated by historical and personal memory. Narita, for instance, was the site of ideological confrontations in the 1960s, whilst

Okinawa was the location of one of the most harrowing battles of the Second World War.

Yet, the film's concerns and the cameraman's voyages extend far beyond the borders of Japan, as Marker seeks to understand how the situation of modern Japan relates to broad global changes in the contemporary world. Hence, it is as a compass point within a field of global relations that Marker explores Japanese culture. Exploiting film's ability to blend different times and places together into a single strand of time, he interweaves film footage from Japan alongside that of Africa, Iceland, France and the United States into an examination of the different forms of economic, ecological and cultural organisation that coexist within the postmodern world. The film therefore constitutes a critical examination of features of the contemporary political and cultural landscape. Through the blending of documentary form and ideological critique with poetic reverie and fiction, Marker provides a subtle and powerful commentary on the plight of non-Western "developing" nations.

Yet, beyond this, *Sunless* is a film about cinema as a conduit for memory and history, and it critically explores the relationship between different forms of representation. Marker is constantly reflecting upon the complexities of the question of the representation and preservation of history in its various manifestations. He is fascinated by the way in which technological media such as audiotape, videotape, photography and film have the ability to "trap" and trigger impressions and memories, yet, in "recording" moments from the past, detach those events from their context or source of origination. This theme acquires added dimensions in respect of the impact of new technologies of image-making. At one point, the commentary states:

> I wonder how people remember things who don't film, don't photograph, don't tape. How has mankind managed to remember? I know, it wrote the Bible. The new Bible will be an eternal magnetic tape of a time that will have to reread itself constantly just to know it existed.

This issue of the fragility of memory saturates the images and commentary throughout the film. The landscape of *Sunless* is an "image world" where cultural memory is scarred by an overriding sense of the "impermanence of things".

As this suggests, the pathway taken in *Sunless* is not straightforward, but a journey through the labyrinth of time and memory. In one respect, the history which Marker relays is a collective history of events, sites and places, but, pervading this is an history made up of personal memories. In the course of the film, the cameraman reflects on his recollections of the political struggles of the past, and on the different aims and strategies of representation that have informed his filmmaking, frequently invoking and re-examining the sounds, themes and images of his previous films and those films, such as Hitchcock's *Vertigo* (1958), that have left their mark on his work. Constructed from letters, impressions, quotations, images and film footage from around the globe, *Sunless* mixes together diverse materials: Marker's own footage, both old and new, but also the "odds and ends" of other films, interweaving these fragments into a complex and fragile whole.

## Epistolary form and characterisation

An important aspect of the presentation of *Sunless* is its use of an epistolary form of narration, a convention Marker had utilised in his films of the 1950s. Yet, the relatively straightforward use of this form in his previous works is, in *Sunless*, overlaid with more complex dimensions. Whilst in *Lettre de Sibérie* (*Letter from Siberia*, 1958) Marker had constructed the commentary in the first person, opening the film with the words "I write to you", *Sunless* opens in the third person, with a female enunciator stating "He wrote me".[2] The film consists of a spoken monologue by this unnamed enunciator, who reads and occasionally comments upon fragments of letters sent to her by a similarly unnamed correspondent whom we know from the beginning to be a freelance cameraman, but who remains unnamed until the end.[3] The letters of the cameraman range from specific impressions and reflections upon images, places and events he encounters on his travels, to observations about his planned or aborted film projects, or his recollections of the past and speculations about the future.

Although this anonymity creates a degree of impersonality, the effect is, in certain respects, arguably more intimate than if the correspondent and enunciator were named. Names here could only be obstructive. This refusal of appellation means that the thoughts conveyed by the enunciator imply a sense of confidentiality, and we are thereby drawn into a close and probing relationship to the correspondence. Bereft of any knowledge about the relationship between the correspondents, the viewer is induced to listen all the more attentively to what is said, and to reconstruct the protagonists out of the fragments we are given. This has the effect of concentrating attention onto the grain of the voice, its subtle inflections and the thoughts they convey, as opposed to who and in what context these words are specifically addressed.

Although laconic, the reflections of the cameraman are composed out of a wide array of forms of address, from candid confessions and concrete observations to more abstract musings. The emotional register is similarly consciously varied, moving rapidly between witty asides and ironical perceptions to more sardonic and even embittered reflections. However, a persistently intimate and questioning tone prevails, frequently drawn towards melancholy and disenchantment, as the cameraman reflects on the course of history, and vainly tries to separate out the mutable appearances of history from its realities. This mutability and ambivalence constitute the intellectual and emotional core of the film, and even appear to extend to the film's characters. As the film progresses, the relationship between the cameraman and his correspondent becomes subtly intertwined. Indeed, at times, it is impossible to decide whether certain observations belong to the cameraman or to the correspondent. Marker creates an effect of "indeterminacy" within the structure of enunciation, embedding observations between the two; in doing so, he creates a fluid interchange between direct and indirect speech, and between the spoken and written word.[4]

This ambiguous status that Marker establishes between the cameraman and the enunciator extends to all the major "characters" named within the film. We can never be entirely confident about ascribing to any of these characters an unequivocal identity. Those familiar with Marker's films will inevitably identify him with the character of the cameraman, and may well recognise that some of the fragments of footage ascribed to this character are taken from Marker's previous films. The cameraman's trips to Guinea-Bissau, Cape Verde, Iceland, the United States, France and Japan mirror the travels of Marker himself, and again, like Marker, he is a maker of political films, who has an affinity for cats and owls, whose emblematic images are dispersed throughout the film. Yet, as if to unsettle the viewer's confidence in such identifications, in the credits the letters of the cameraman are ascribed to "Sandor Krasna". Similarly, the film's electronic sounds are attributed to "Michel Krasna". This again has its own ironies and associations. The surname "Krasna" may be interpreted as shorthand for "Krasnapolski", one of Marker's fictional family names.[5]

In addition, another "unseen" character in the course of the film enticingly evokes characteristics associated with Marker.[6] "Hayao Yamaneko" uses computer technology to alter, edit and transform images graphically from an historical archive of film footage. The cameraman ruminates on several occasions on "his friend"'s digitalised representations of the past, and, at certain points, images from the film itself recur, reworked through Yamaneko's technology. Once again, those familiar with Marker's recent experiments with video and computer technology will recognise the "signature" of Marker himself on Yamaneko's images, and may recognise footage used in his previous film, *Le Fond de l'air est rouge* (1977).[7] In the light of this, it is tempting to see each of the characters that emerge within the film as *alter egos* for Marker, externalising, augmenting and separating out different, even conflicting aspects of his own personality.[8] Taken as such, these characters afford Marker the opportunity for both self-assertion and self-effacement, the latter a quality he admires in Japanese culture.[9]

Yet, one should resist the temptation to see these characters as simply aggregates of Marker. Just as the use of the female voice to enunciate the cameraman's reflections always holds us at one remove from the identity of the cameraman, so these characters act as "mediating points of reference" that perpetually hold open the gap between Marker's own identity and that of the reflections of the characters.[10]

Marker's reticence about "who speaks" in *Sunless* indicates both a self-conscious examination of the rhetorical modes of construction of autobiography, and an unwillingness to speak of his past as if it were simply present to consciousness.[11] To speak of the self that one once was is to risk ignoring the role of forgetfulness in memory, to erase all that which eludes the present moment from which one speaks. It is, in short, to abstract that "other" self from the midst of the material world of the past in which it was embodied. Without falling prey to "hermeneutic nihilism", Marker, at each turn, questions our access to the past, posing a series of questions about the complex nature of referentiality.[12] Hence, in examining the anteriority of the past, Marker is led to interrogate the nature of self-representation.

These characters therefore provide Marker with the opportunity to disperse observations, and thereby to enlarge and complicate the perspective of the film. In the light of this, it may also be salutary to remember that "Marker" is itself a pseudonym, and that Marker has described *Sunless* as an interweaving of materials that forges a collective fictional memory.[13] Consistent with this, the scenes included in the film freely interweave fragments of the work of other filmmakers not only in the form of quotation, but also as part of the raw material out of which the film is composed. We see scenes from Sana na N'hada's *Carnival in Bissau*, Mario Marret and Eugenio Bentivoglio's *Guerrilla in Bissau*, Jean-Michel Humeau's *Ranks Ceremony*, Danièle Tessier's *Death of a Giraffe* and Haroun Tazieff's *Iceland 1970*, which are interspersed with Marker's own footage with little or no attention being drawn to the suturing between original and borrowed materials.[14] Similarly, an array of fragments of video film and televisual materials are scattered like a mosaic throughout *Sunless*. Through such juxtapositions and ambiguous characterisations, Marker undermines any notion of a "self-contained subject", implying that memory and the subjectivity from which memory itself is born are likewise perpetually reconstructed out of diverse materials.

Beyond complicating common notions of the subject, the contingent forms of *Sunless* establish an intricate and finely balanced contrapuntal structure. The film's montage of images creates a universal breadth, intermixing footage that has no single unifying characteristic. An initial disorientation occurs, as we rapidly cut across different cultures, times and places. The consistency that is achieved by having one enunciator reading the reflections of the absent cameraman reasserts a provisional continuity and unity to the film that counterbalance the effect of the radical montage technique.[15] A rhythmic counterpoint is therefore set up between the sonorous cadences of the voice, which become familiar as the film progresses, and the more frenetic waves of images and sounds. Yet, this continuity is itself complicated by the way in which a counterpoint is established between the enunciation, whose references to the letters are framed within the past tense ("He wrote me"), and the images which often induce a sense of "presentness" between the filmmaker's observations and what is shown onscreen.

In sum, Marker's modes of presentation within the film represent a critical engagement with the question of representation itself. A more flexible approach to the characterisations within *Sunless* would therefore be to see these characters as "positions" within the film which are mobilised to a variety of structural, as well as autobiographical ends. Hence, "Yamaneko'"s modes of imaging provide a counterpoint to "Krasna'"s camerawork. They represent alternate approaches to representation, alternate aesthetics and alternate strategies to the question of the representation of memory which are deployed in the course of the film, and which at various moments Marker himself has deployed. *Sunless* is therefore neither entirely fictional nor entirely autobiographical, but exists at the interface of these categories.[16]

## Image and sound

*Sunless* dispenses with many of the conventions that traditionally structure films. The work has little in the way of plot or chronological development, and similarly – although occasional sequences of "arbitrarily" positioned narrative filter into the film – there is ultimately nothing that could be classified as a story-line in any conventional sense. Instead, images, anecdotes, fragments of letters and sketches for projects emerge, trail off and re-emerge in unexpected ways. The classical unities of time and place are constantly interrupted as the film traverses different places and different times, bringing them into a dialectical relationship with each other. At times, the kaleidoscopic nature of the film may convey a sense of randomness and even disorientation for the spectator, who searches in vain for the familiar footholds of the conventions of traditional narrative cinema. Marker insists that his audience dispense with these structures and adapt to a different way of reading. The viewer has to respond to shifting modes of signification, and read the film according to both diachronic and synchronic modes of reading, constantly referring to what has gone before and reappraising its significance. Hence, to come to terms with the film requires one to follow the film's complex "pathways", to attend closely to the style of Marker's presentation which is inextricable from its content.

An essential feature of the originality and challenging nature of *Sunless* is the form in which it unfolds its themes. Themes do not emerge sequentially but cyclically, discreetly arising out of subtle correspondences and repetitions that the edits establish in the course of the film.[17] Marker consciously and consistently undermines any clear hierarchical structure of the film's elements, replacing this with a more democratic form of "shifting dominants", in which each moment of the film acquires a relative equality. This pertains even to the presentation of key imagery within the film. Although, as the film progresses, certain recurring images become of particular importance in the elaboration of the film's themes – for example, the imagery of destruction and death (images of fire, natural disasters and the disasters of war), and most especially the imagery of the sea (a metaphor which carries many connotations in the film: memory, flux, death and infinitude) – there is no attempt immediately to impose the larger significance of this imagery within the film upon the viewer's consciousness. Many of the most poignant images appear and disappear from the screen in a matter of seconds, whilst other less plangent moments may prevail for a longer duration. Only through an acute attentiveness to the associations that arise out of the juxtapositions of commentary and images and the reoccurrences of certain structural units of the film does the viewer begin to decipher the significance of particular passages and their bearing on the film as a whole.

The momentum of the film thus centres on the free-flowing juxtapositions of images and the suggestive relationships of continuity and discontinuity which these establish with the soundtrack and commentary. Marker's editing is exceptionally intricate, establishing subtle and complex relations between the diverse components of his film. This is by no means straightforward. The film's continuity is constantly interrupted by Marker's interconnecting of fragments of images, binding together footage from his travels across the globe and footage from different moments in time in a way that stresses the mutability of their significance. The images snatched from these moments and places, displaced from their original context, are stitched together into a series of sequences of varying length and tempo that establish intricate rhythms, visual harmonies and counterpoints within the film, and create gradual and sometimes abrupt changes in mood, subject-matter and location.

Marker's editing does not follow a uniform pattern. Some edits proceed by theme, and some by association in *bricolage* fashion or by structural opposition, whilst others proceed according to formal requirements, which correspond to such criteria as the position of the images within the frame, screen direction and camera angle. Often what seem to be random shots of the mundane are carefully contrived to achieve a particular aesthetic effect. Characteristically, Marker utilises the whole expanse of the screen, editing the flow of images with an eye to formal symmetry and contrast. In the spectacular scenes of the neighbourhood celebrations in Tokyo, for instance, Marker tracks the dancing and parading figures across the entire length of the screen, having figures that exit from one side of the screen be replaced by others entering from the other side, and vice versa. Alternatively, in a passage that follows the journey of a train in Tokyo, he edits together groups of shots from different perspectives, which, like a Cubist painting, present the object of attention simultaneously from an array of alternative points of view.

Indeed, in *Sunless*, Marker demonstrates his mastery of the range of technical possibilities of montage. Through his editing, he develops variable logics which may be at work within even a single edit. This creates a high degree of semantic instability, with the result that single images and sequences become polyphonic, acquiring multiple significance and resonances on different planes of meaning as the film progresses. Many of these edits are structured around the interplay of motion and stillness, the basic rhythms of cinema. In one passage, synthesised images of a kamikaze plane are replaced by footage of the wing of a contemporary jet flying high above Africa. This, in turn, is followed by dogs trailing across the waterline of a sandy beach and a striking overhead shot of desert dunes whose surface resembles the rolling patterns of waves of the previous shot. In the final moment of this sequence, another overhead shot, an African woman gazes from the deck of a boat out over the waves of the sea. The freeze-framing of her face both recalls and links up to other sequences in which Marker focuses on the reciprocal interchange of gazes between subject (cameraman) and object (those whom he films), and brings the interplay of sequences of images of stillness and motion to a temporary halt.

In another sequence that again centres on the interplay of moments of animation with moments of stillness, the statue of a camel in Africa is succeeded by a mannequin of a policeman, replete with white gloves, strategically positioned on the bend of a road near Japan's Shiba coast in order to discourage speeding. This, in turn, is followed by a cut to a close-up on the white gloves of a Japanese bus driver. Through the windows of the mobile bus, we see shots of a scarecrow which satirically echoes the mannequin of the policeman, a pile of abandoned "junked" cars, and an aeroplane parked in a carnival, images whose suspension of animation contrasts with the mobility of the bus, and which return us to the stillness of the statues that opened the sequence.[18] Whilst this pattern of editing establishes a certain containment of these elements within a coherent structure, the imagery in this sequence also extends beyond its initial context to echo and link up with other images of travel, policing, statues, débris and wastelands that appear earlier and later in the film. In another passage, footage of an African heron prompts, by way of a free association on the part of the commentary, a cut to an emu in the Ile-de-France. The camera then focuses in on the eye of the emu, then cuts first to the gaze of an African woman and then to the eye of the recurring motif of the votive Japanese figurine of a cat. These images of the eye link up through the course of the film with a host of other images of the eye, and become linked in the commentaries to themes of power, surveillance, voyeurism, representation and the magical function of the eye (both the actual eye and the "camera eye") in non-Western cultures.

As these sequences suggest, Marker's employment of a montage technique, whilst bearing its own very distinctive traits, astutely draws on the innovations of Soviet monteurs such as Vertov, Kulešov, Eisenstein and Medvedkin. The dialectical use of montage editing in early Soviet cinema to carry and consolidate a cinematographic message across a progression of images is utilised by Marker in a number of sequences in suggestive ways.[19] For instance, in one passage which explores the relationship of the sacred and the profane, we are lead from pornographic images on late-night Japanese television, via a succession of advertising posters for an exhibition of the Vatican's treasures in Tokyo, to a Hokkaido departmental store which, as the commentary remarks, combines the functions of sex shop, chapel and museum. These posters feature the outstretched arms of Pope John Paul II, and it is the recurrence of these posters which take us from the exterior streets of the city to the interior of the Vatican exhibition. These images accompany the commentary's contrast of the alternate attitudes to sexuality within Western and Eastern religions, and a provocative commentary that links censorship on the "adult" channels on Japanese television with Christian dogma.

Whilst these examples demonstrate Marker's use of editing to control tightly the unfolding of a sequence, his editing often veers in an opposite direction. Fragments of footage are often purposefully displaced, Marker sharply intercutting images in a way that defers their meaning. For instance, although the footage of an Apollo space rocket seen near the beginning of the film is not entirely devoid of significance in the initial context in which it appears, it does not fully connect to the film's imagery until close to the film's conclusion. Only then is it mentioned that the Apollo astronauts trained at a site in Iceland devastated by a volcanic irruption, the site we recognise as where the film's initial footage of children is set. This connection is then augmented by the use of this site as the setting of a sketch for a science-fiction story. Equally, the images of the broken figurine of a votive cat upon which Marker fixes his gaze acquire significance only in respect of the later images of ruins and dismembered bodies.

Moreover, not all the edits are intended to advance analysis. Some set up subtle and even whimsical conceits characteristic of Marker's cinema. In one sequence, the commentary remarks on the fact that, in the Bijago, it is the women who chose their husbands. We then cut from the profile of a young Bijago woman staring intently leftwards, to a row of the aforementioned Japanese votive cat figurines, all of whom have one arm raised as if vying for contention for her affections. Similarly, there are moments when Marker's camera lingers on something for the sheer pleasure that its appearance provides. In the carnival scenes in Tokyo, he scrutinises the intense concentration upon the face of one of the dancers.

Throughout the film, there is a constant interplay of different levels of representation, and this again motivates Marker's editing. For instance, actual film footage of trains is intercut with animated footage of trains from the popular Japanese "Manga" cartoon; the sequence of the slaughter of the giraffe by hunters begins with a television segment in which a figure fires a pistol; and footage of, among other things, political demonstrations dematerialises and rematerialises in turn as it is filtered through the digitalised technology of the "zone". By constantly shifting between different levels of representation, Marker is able, through his editing, to create a dialogue between them, to examine their different modes of signification and how they connect to each other.

As this implies, Marker uses a montage technique to create echoes and counterpoints between images which alternately reinforce, contradict or intensify each other. Any one sequence or series of images may establish an array of relationships as the film progresses.

Marker's eye for ironic and telling juxtapositions allows him to obtain the maximum amount of diversity and fluidity without losing the sense of structure. Plangent images of pain and even death intermingle with images of tenderness and joy; images of the sacred are interwoven with the erotic and profane; the exotic with the mundane; forlorn hopelessness with images of struggle and resistance. These juxtapositions and the themes that emerge out of them, although grounded in concrete circumstances, begin to forge correspondences that transcend time and place, blurring distinctions between moments and places. In one sequence, for instance, we move from a lighthouse on the Cape Verde island of Sal by way of a graphic match with a ruined tower of Montepilloy in France, both of which are compared with a long January shadow of a bonze located in a Tokyo plaza. This is one of many passages in which Marker links up three continents simultaneously. In the course of the film, we slip from a shoreline in California to a shoreline in Iceland, from images of demonstrations at Narita in Japan in the 1960s and 1980s to anticolonial demonstrations in Portugal, and from the battleground of the island of Okinawa to the battlegrounds of the war of liberation in Guinea-Bissau.

The film's method is therefore to search for the discreet connections between seemingly disparate times and places, and also to allow juxtapositions of images to resonate suggestively without necessarily having a clearly prefixed meaning. Yet, this search for correspondences is counterbalanced by a logic of dissociation. Although, in *Sunless*, image and enunciation often provide explicit commentary on each other, they do not always correspond. Rather than hierarchically subordinating images to words, Marker sets up an intricate dialogue between them. The cameraman's text skims across images and vice versa, opening up possible meanings or even suggesting "gaps" of meaning.

The opening sequence that precedes the titles is exemplary of the complexities of the relationship Marker establishes between the commentary, the images and other components of the film. The film opens with a black leader over which the enunciator states: "the first image he told me about was of three children on a road in Iceland in 1965". For a few seconds we then see this serene silent footage of three blonde children walking in a scenic Icelandic landscape, filmed in bright sunlight, which has the artless simplicity and intimacy of a "home-movie", after which the black leader returns and the enunciator continues: "He said that for him it was the image of happiness, and also that he had tried several times to link it to other images, but it never worked". As the enunciator speaks, the black leader is interrupted for a few seconds by acquired footage of a United States war-plane descending into the bowels of an aircraft carrier, an image that receives no commentary and is succeeded again by black leader and the comment, "He wrote me: 'One day I'll have to put it all alone at the beginning of a film...If they [viewers] don't see happiness in the picture, at least they'll see the black'". After which the opening titles, including the title of the film, appear. This dialectical juxtaposition immediately shifts the emotional register from serenity to disquiet, and may even be read as contradicting the commentary's earlier remark about the cameraman's intentions to place this footage of happiness "all alone at the beginning of a film".[20]

As the film progresses, Marker augments the meanings of this allusive sequence in later sequences that echo and repeat the initial pairing of childhood with the armoury of war. In the first, we move from an image of a child in Japan to a child in Africa, via footage of a Polaris missile. In the second, we return to the opening footage of the children in Iceland in its entirety, although its return, as if by memory, is subtly changed. Now there is a slightly blurred ending, and the "shaky frame", which had been "tidied up" in the first presentation of the footage in order to make the sequence more accomplished, is now allowed to stand, testifying to the strong wind and the filmmaker's complete absorption in the subject he was filming.[21] In the meantime, a volcano on the island has irrupted and, as the scenes succeeding this reappearance of the footage reveal, the village where the footage was taken has partially disappeared under the lava and ashes. In the third recurrence of this imagery of the children in Iceland, we see the footage transformed through Yamaneko's "zone". The transference of the original footage to the zone marks a passage from one order of the representation to another, the transformation of the indexical image to that of the "zone's abstractions".

In each of these sequences, a certain melancholy prevails. In the first two recurrences, this occurs via the juxtaposition with forces of nuclear and natural destruction. In the latter, melancholy arises on account of the loss of the phenomenal presence of the image as it is transmuted by Yamaneko's technology. In retrospect, the black leader following the opening shots, far from being simply an empty "negative" space, acquires the status of being a sign which comes to stand for the collective experiences of loss and destruction, all the allusions to finality and death that the film evokes and which ultimately threaten the collective memory of civilisation.

Characteristically, Marker's juxtapositions seek to suggest connections and to open, rather than close down, discussion. In one of the most intricate sequences, he uses "channel-hopping" on late-night Japanese television both to establish a *mise en abime* of his own montage editing technique, and to create a poignant montage of images which are richly evocative. During this sequence, the cameraman turns from one channel featuring a programme on the Enlightenment philosopher Jean-Jacques Rousseau to another which features images of the genocide perpetrated by the Khmer Rouge in Cambodia. The latter is accompanied on the soundtrack by Kurtz's monologue from *Apocalypse Now* (1979), after which the commentary states: "From Jean-Jacques Rousseau to the Khmer Rouge. Coincidence or the sense of history?".

As this sequence continues, the film suggests how a certain accumulation of recurrent images on late-night Japanese television, mainly of Japanese popular Sumari and horror films, taken together may be read as a text that allegorises certain patterns of social and sexual stratification, desire and power. Probing beneath the surface flow of the images, Marker invokes the memories of the history of the past of the Asian peoples and the subjugations of the present that are encoded in such imagery, and further comments on both the deeper unconscious significance that images of horror play within Japanese society, and, related to this, the extraordinary aestheticisation of horror in Japanese culture. Following this commentary, stills from Japanese horror movies are rapidly intercut with other stills from erotic and pornographic movies, and with the kind of advertising images featuring women seen earlier in the sequence. The juxtapositions of these stills suggestively draws out the persistence of certain ideological notions and cultural divisions within and across gender categories. Beyond the specific significance these images have in relation to the Asian continent, in the course of the film these images of horror, desire and power become connected to the actual horrors of the footage of the victims of the wars, the meditation on the subjugation of women across different continents, and other questions about representation which Marker evokes throughout the course of the film.

Through the form of *Sunless*, Marker induces a critical dialogue between the film and its viewers, forcing the viewer to become active in interpreting the significance of what is being shown, and to ponder on the film's juxtapositions, rather than passively relying upon the commentary to communicate their significance. And it is the fragment that forms the kernel of this endeavour. This concern with instigating a reflective consciousness, rather than simply conveying a message, is also vividly apparent in the general form of the observations of the commentary. The fragments of the cameraman's letters are mostly anecdotal and epigrammatical – indeed, even aphoristic on occasion – stimulating reflection, rather than closing down meaning.

This is not to say, however, that Marker's editing lacks a common purpose. What ultimately structures the various parts of the film is the concern to find a form of presentation that approximates the associative faculties of memory. The various patterns of the edits interweave image and sound in a way that is analogous to the structure of reflective consciousness. The varying length of shot and dissolve often seems to respond to the demand of memory: the lingering of a memory, for instance, or its sudden termination and replacement by other images and thoughts that are evoked by way of reflective association and even dissociation. This extends to the viewer's experience of Marker's montage technique, which appeals to the flow of undirected or reflective thought, to thought that is not narrowly channelled but is associational, the very thought patterns which we identify with memory.

Moreover, the dynamic structure of signification may also be read as reflecting the workings of memory. The recurring of images and sequences in different series not only enriches their significance, but also transforms them through their perpetual recontextualisation. In this way, the succession of images seems to mirror the ebb and flow of a consciousness that is continually pervaded by the memories of the past; memories which will never remain stable, but exist in a state of becoming, on account of the fact that their reappearance always recurs within the ever-changing context of the present.[22]

This experience of memory as constantly reconfigured by consciousness is integral to the film's evocation of melancholy. For the experience of the past, as a shifting field of relations, invokes a sense of abjection.[23] Not only are the reflections and images of the cameraman presented as fragments that can never be wholly defined or reconstituted, but also the often rapid succession of images induces a sense of fragility. As Yvette Biro has astutely remarked, Marker's "glitteringly fine observations" press the viewer "to the verge of straining [their] receptivity":[24]

> [Marker] recreates...the vertigo of time. In each moment [of the film] there is struggle: we try to preserve the experiences we have had, storing them in the fragile warehouse of our memory. However, the recordings we have fade too fast, losing their poignancy under the corrosion of time. But here exactly lies the triumphant paradox of Marker's beautiful film. The mind might be powerless in the unequal struggle with time, but not in revealing, forcefully, the story of this dramatic loss.[25]

The figure of the spiral, which, as we will see, becomes an essential motif in *Sunless*, ultimately shapes the form of the film's unfolding. As the work draws to a close, we begin to see that the progression of the film takes the form of an ever-diminishing spiral, where sequences and images recur in ever-changed form and with ever-greater rapidity.

Perhaps the key to Marker's approach in composing *Sunless* lies in a reference made early on in the film to the work of Sei Shōnagon, the female Japanese writer and diarist of the Heian period.[26] Sei Shōnagon's famous *Makura no sōshi* (*The Pillow Book*, c.886-1000) is a vast and miscellaneous collection of *zuhitsu*, personal notes and occasional writings mostly compiled during her time as lady-in-waiting to Empress Sadako during the last decade of the 10th century. *The Pillow Book* is widely held to be not only a consummately crafted work of prose, but also one of the most important historical documents of the mid-Heian period. Today it survives only in fragmentary form, a montage of impressions, character sketches, anecdotes and acute observations on nature, objects and the everyday life of the court. It is the 164 lists that Sei Shōnagon composed within *The Pillow Book* that are of most interest to Marker; lists such as "Things that arouse a fond memory of the past", "Elegant things", "Rare things", "Distressing things" or "Things that quicken the heart". Such lists – and the latter in particular, to which, at one point, the commentary refers, over a tracking shot of the ascent of a Polaris missile – might be seen as analogous to Marker's own project in *Sunless*.[27] Indeed, there are numerous explicit and implicit references to Sei Shōnagon's lists. The reference at the beginning of the film to the list of "things that quicken the heart" in retrospect can be seen to refer to the use of an amplified heartbeat in the soundtrack during the sequence on the Hokkaido ferry, or to resonate in the light of the grotesque and distressing footage of the slaughter that we see in the film. We might therefore regard Sei Shōnagon's book as providing a literary counterpart to Marker's film, and regard Marker as reaching back into the distant memory of Japanese culture to discover the model for his own visual exploration of the everyday life of contemporary Japanese culture. *The Pillow Book* serves Marker as an example of an alternative mode of representing history and a model for organising his filmic impressions. Not only does it provide a "method" – the commentary refers to Sei Shōnagon's lists as providing a useful criterion of selection when filming – but also we sense the commentary's reflections about the disenfranchisement from political influence that gave rise to such writings, as Sei Shōnagon's echoes the sensibility of the filmmaker, weary of the "intransigence" of history to the cause of social and political justice. Hence, the commentary's description of the prose stylists of the Heian period might also, in certain respects, be applicable to Marker's own contemplation of the signs of everyday existence:

> By learning to draw a sort of melancholy comfort from the contemplation of the tiniest things, this small group of idlers left a mark on Japanese sensibility much deeper than the mediocre thundering of the politicians.

Any discussion of composition and mode of address in *Sunless* needs to take into account not only the relation between the commentary and the images, but also the relation of the soundtrack to these elements. Indeed, there is an important analogy to be drawn between the polyphonic form of Marker's montage and certain forms of musical structure. As with musical structure, the film has to be grasped intuitively as a whole, rather than sequentially part-by-part or note-by-note. Furthermore, Marker stated his aim of weaving the various filmic elements of *Sunless* into "[t]he fashion of a musical composition, with recurrent themes, counterpoints and mirror like fugues".[28] Marker develops his film-fugue contrapuntally, by way of a four-part invention of speech and image, sound and silence. The contribution of the latter two to the film's total effect should not be underestimated. Like the voids in Japanese prints and Chinese scrolls, or the pauses in musical progression, the silences in *Sunless* are often as telling and weighted as the commentary. As with the use of ironic juxtapositions of images, music plays an important role in provoking thought and establishing the tenor of *Sunless*. In a manner comparable to Godard's experiments with soundtrack, music is employed not simply to augment the images (for example, imitating the rhythms of travel or crowds) or to set the mood, but as an important element of the film in its own right.

Indeed, Marker creates a many-faceted relationship between image, sound and commentary, using music to create a vivid set of allusions.[29] The music used in *Sunless* is very varied, bringing together, and even intermingling, heterogeneous musical forms. These include traditional, classical and folk music from different periods and different regions, including Asia, Africa and Europe, and many other musical forms. This diverse array of music, some of which belongs to the realm of traditional and sacred rituals, and some to the world of commodified leisure, collides and jars with each other, like a schemata of conflicting languages. In turn, these musical forms periodically mingle with industrial noise, the hubbub of video games, advertising jingles, and the sounds and rhythms generated in everyday city life. Hence, although the use of music frequently serves to locate places through the invocation of musical forms indigenous to them, music is as often employed to create overlaps between the often abrupt transitions from one place and time to another.

The music in *Sunless* also serves to evoke moments from the past that constantly filter into the present, breaking up the continuity in time. To take some instances: in one sequence, images of Guinea-Bissau are accompanied by music from the Cape Verde islands while the enunciator comments on the filmmaker's request for this juxtaposition as a symbolic tribute to the goal of Amilcar Cabral of uniting the two countries. In another sequence in a bar in Tokyo, the soundtrack plays a musical refrain from *La Jetée* (1962), invoking the way in which sound can be the conduit of memory, and can establish discreet intertextual references to other films. Similarly, at certain points in time, music used in one sequence recurs in another in order to announce the return of particular themes. For example, the music accompanying the ceremonies of mourning the death of a panda recurs just prior to, and then during, the scene of the violent slaughter of a giraffe.

Gradually, in the course of the film, one becomes aware of how these various sounds, like the film's images, are filtered through a synthesiser which distorts their original sound (i.e. sound is given a rippled effect or slowed down). Like the "zone" which translates memories into "pure" images, so the synthesiser music transforms the array of different musical forms into "pure sound", flattening the distinctions between them.

The role of music within the soundtrack is therefore interwoven into the thematics of the film. The film derives its title from a six-part melancholic song-cycle by Mussorgsky, and Marker's technique uses counterpoint and repetition to announce themes in a way that parallels Mussorgsky's music. Although only a brief fragment of Mussorgsky's cycle of songs (a passage from "Sur le fleuve", the last of the songs in the cycle, which concerns itself with death) is heard in the course of the film, Marker uses the song cycle as a vehicle to establish his leitmotif of the fragility of memory. In the *mise en abîme* sequence set in the year 4001 (explored later in this book), the theme about memory and forgetting centres upon the "lost associations" of the Mussorgsky composition.

Beyond such explicit references, Marker creates a series of discreet dialogues between the film and the song cycle, thereby establishing a hypertextual relationship between the two. On a formal level, both works display an amazing richness in compositional conventions and expressive possibilities, but use extremely economic means to achieve these aims. However, *Sunless* shares more than simply formal compositional affinities with Mussorgsky's song cycle. They share an extensive common range of imagery and a common mood of melancholy.

Any list of these would include the following: imaginative re-creations of the events of long ago; introspective, even bitter and regretful musings on the past and the present, which, as in *Sunless*, are also addressed to an unnamed female correspondent; the imagery of crowds; an accentuation on the *impression* and the fleeting moment; the experience of frustration and ennui; a self-consciousness of the passing of time; distant happiness, hidden hopes and mournful, regretful thoughts; the interweaving of images of wakefulness and sleep; a shifting between figures of nature with those of the city; the imagery of "deep waters" and intimations of death. This imagery constitutes an extensive common "topography" between Marker's film and Mussorgsky's composition.

Time, place and memory

*Sunless* is prefaced by a quotation from T S Eliot's poem, "Ash-Wednesday" (1930):

> Because I know that time is always time
> And place is always and only place[30]

This allusion prepares the way for the radical undermining of conventional notions of time and place in *Sunless*. At the commencement of the film, we witness a journey, a return by ferry from the island of Hokkaido to the metropolis of Tokyo, but this journey is not simply a journey in time, from place to place, but a journey about time and about place. We are aware from the beginning that the journeys we are tracking come to us in the form of fragments of memory. The fragments of these journeys do not unfold linearly, making it impossible to reconstitute the journeys in chronological order, or to gauge the temporal span of the journey. The paths trodden are those of a traveller revisiting once more sites and places previously visited. On the cameraman's arrival in Tokyo, we are hurriedly taken on a tour of his favourite haunts of the past.[31] These journeys are continually interwoven with images from the past and from other places, Marker brilliantly exploiting the full potentiality of cinema as a vehicle for the representation of subjective memory. Cinema's capacity to transcend the concrete limitations of time and place allows Marker to juxtapose and interweave fragments of images, events and sounds taken from around the globe, in a manner that approximates the patterns of reflective consciousness.

The images of these travels are therefore grounded in a particular memory ever-present in the idiosyncratic choices of sites and spectacles, which frequently recall the staple elements of Marker's previous films. Equally, from the very beginning, a particular sensibility, redolent with its own prehistory, permeates the film. As we watch the footage of passengers on the Hokkaido ferry, the enunciator, reading from the letters of the cameraman, comments:

> I've been round the world several times, and now only banality still interests me. On this trip, I've tracked it with the relentlessness of a bounty hunter.

Yet, if "banality" constitutes Marker's stated field of investigation, what *Sunless* reveals is the extraordinary world lurking within the quotidian life of the metropolis, the signs of unconscious desire and collective dreams encoded within the banal.

As the cameraman surveys Tokyo, what is initially conveyed are the rhythms and "crush of signs" encountered in the city. Marker's editing in this sequence, in its creation of abrupt and constantly shifting viewpoints from street level to rooftop, conveys a sense of simultaneity, the camerawork re-creating an effect of fleeting glances scanning the city for its characteristic signs. These signs shuttle forth in rapid succession, some immediately decipherable, some less so, with little in the way of guidance for the viewer. In this way, Marker captures both the sense of exhilaration and seductive allure that the encounter with the city provides, and the strange sense of fragmentation, illegibility and disarticulation.[32] Tracking images of crowds descending the stairs of the subway, the commentary suggests that the city should be deciphered like a complex "musical score", one in which "one could get lost in the great orchestral masses and the accumulation of detail". The city's form is always therefore on the brink of formlessness.[33] Marker draws out this sense of disarticulation by way of revealing juxtapositions. Moving from one part of the city to next, he catalogues the clash of historical references and quotation of the architecture and public works adorning the streets. In one of the most revealing of these juxtapositions, one which creates an extraordinary sense of historical density, Marker films the statue of a Buddha in a cemetery overlooking the network of train lines that form the city's nerve centre.

Initially, the image-saturated Japanese metropolis is represented as a delirious and fraught "world of appearances", a dystopian 20th-century equivalent of the "floating world" of the Edo period, a metaphor which finds its concrete embodiment in the shots of the many advertising placards of beautiful young Japanese models suspended in mid-air over the city, hanging from invisible wires and cables above the streets and railway lines which cut through the city. This intoxicating realm of advertising and the mass media invades public space and private thought alike.[34] Here the omnipresent video and television screens that adorn the department store walls, the computer-generated images, and the huge, Western-style advertising billboards and murals taken from the comic strip books hail to and prevail upon the passer-by, dwarfing them with their monumental scale. There is more than a suggestion in such imagery of the way in which the modern city acquires the character of a space of surveillance. The huge images adorning the city's billboards, featuring figures looking out of the posters, cast their gaze across the city, "voyeurising the voyeurs".[35] Equally, the erotically-charged images of young women and comic-strip heroines, on a scale inflated out of all proportion, seem starkly to counterpoint the impersonality, constraint and conformity that reign over the street-life below, as though they were the projections of repressed desires. In one of the most telling images, the reflections of a mass of figures in the subway are absorbed within the giant billboard image of a fashion model.

Ultimately, we are shown that, in this postmodern megalopolis, reality and dreams are inextricable from each other, as representation becomes determining of reality. Following the sequence where the cameraman scans Japanese late-night television with its plethora of images of desire, horror and violence, the scene shifts to the subterranean tunnels that lead from the department store malls to the train stations. In the course of this sequence, Marker invokes the long-standing trope of the train, both as metaphor for the cinematic apparatus and as symbol of industrial progress. Yet, Marker's invocation of this metaphor reinvents its meanings. Whilst, for the Soviet monteurs, the metaphor of the train was integrally bound up with the image of the progression of history, for Marker, in the context of Tokyo's postmodernity, it becomes a metaphor for a society given over to forms of visual spectacle:[36]

> More and more, my dreams find their settings in the department stores of Tokyo, the subterranean tunnels that extend them and run parallel to the city. A face appears, disappears, a trace is found, is lost, all the folklore of dreams is so much in its place that the next day, when I'm awake, I realise that I continue to seek in the basement labyrinth the presence concealed the night before. I begin to wonder if those dreams are really mine, or if they are part of a totality, of a gigantic collective dream of which the entire city may be the projection. It might suffice to pick up any one of the telephones that are lying around to hear a familiar voice, or the beating of a heart – Sei Shōnagon's for example... All the galleries lead to stations, the same companies own the

stores and the railroads that bear their name, Kelo, Odakyu, all those names of ports. The train inhabited by sleeping people puts together all the fragments of dreams, makes a single film of them, the ultimate film. The tickets from the automatic dispenser grant admission to the show.

The images which accompany this commentary show commuters buying tickets for the subway (images that invoke the queues of spectators buying tickets for admission to the cinema), boarding train compartments, and, once seated, drifting into sleep, a segment which recalls and brings full circle the journey into the city in the film's opening passages. As this sequence progresses, images of the passengers' sleeping faces are allusively intercut with images of the late-night television sequences replayed from the night before, suggesting the way in which these images of desire and violence become imprinted onto their subconscious thoughts and dreams. The passage offers us not only an example of the film's intricate use of montage to slip nimbly between the realms of desire and the everyday, dream and wakefulness, subjective and collective memory, but also an image of a world whose experience of "the real" is, in actuality, constantly and imperceptibly shifting between these categories.[37]

Yet, if at times Marker presents a picture of the city as "overcrowded, megalomaniac, inhuman", he qualifies this by drawing attention to other subtler sides of the city, to the beauty of the reflections of the light in January, to the particularity of the faces and the lives of the twelve million or so inhabitants of the city, "as different and precise as groups of instruments"; or to the ways in which the patterns of everyday existence restructure and reclaim the megalopolis: the way, for instance, that, after dark, the impersonality of the city by day gives way to the transformation of the city into a "series of villages". Marker is sensitive also to the marginal life of the city, to all that disrupts its rational functioning. In one sequence, a homeless alcoholic in a run-down quarter of the Tokyo suburbs assumes the authority of the role of a policeman directing the traffic from the middle of a busy junction. In another, the poorest of the Tokyo poor park themselves in front of television screens in the chic department stores to watch the Sumo contests. These images grow in significance in the light of how tightly coded and hierarchically ordered Japanese society is.

This meditation upon the metropolis of Tokyo becomes interwoven with a series of commentaries on the economic position of Japan, its political landscape, and its complex relations to other continents. Comparing "the battle of integrated circuits" with the battles in the past for territorial conquests, the film asks whether history is now primarily driven by the competition to colonise the global market for technology. Clearly, one of the reasons why Marker returns to Japan is that it has arguably become the leading manufacturer of the new technologies that are transforming our experience of the world. Yet, aside from this, the fascination of Japan for us today is the manner in which the impact of new technologies and Westernisation has not simply eclipsed previous long-standing cultural customs, but coexist with pre-existent cultural patterns, creating a peculiar relationship between modernisation and the perpetuation of tradition. He continually returns throughout the film to various sacred observances and rituals that preserve the practices of the past. Hence, whilst pointing to the rapid changes that have taken place in recent Japanese history, he probes the new cultural forms of modern Japan for symptoms of the deeply encoded patterns of the past. Indeed, Marker's description in *Letter from Siberia* of Siberia as a land of contrasts "situated between the Middle Ages and the 21st century" might provide a fitting epigraph for the analysis of his portrayal of Japan in *Sunless*.

These observations about Japan lead on to a probing examination of the question of the relationship between the "developing Third World" and the West. The film points to the coexistence of very different experiences of modernity within the global economy. Intercutting images of the highly technologised and affluent society of contemporary Japan with images of the rural poor of Africa, a contrast is drawn between the processes of modernisation in Japan and a way of life that involves a daily struggle for survival. These contrasts not only are registered in economic divisions, but also imply a different experience of the temporal and nature. Marker here is keen to undercut any sentimentalising of the rural existence of the "Third World", a vision which is obliquely referenced in the course of the film by way of a succession of images of monuments to Rousseau, his château and its grounds. Instead, he shows its hardships and local struggles as a form of existence almost forgotten by the West.

Marker is concerned, however, to show not only the separation of the "first" and "third worlds", but also the ties that bind such disparate places together. For, in the postmodern world, few borders remain intact. This theme unfolds in the course of the film, initially through images of displacement. Images of "exoticism", indicative of a prior wave of colonialism, are transferred to Europe (i.e. the narrator comments on two occasions about the emus that live in the Ile-de-France, and footage of them recurs on a number of occasions). Similarly, elements of European kitsch and remnants of European culture are shown to pervade Asia and Africa. Later, this traversing of boundaries is made more explicit in a sequence where the cameraman comments on a short-wave radio announcement projected to Tokyo that is picked up on a Cape Verde island.

Moreover, as we are shuttled back and forth between the pre-industrialised landscape of Africa and the "post-industrialised" economy of Japan, we become aware not only of the disparities between the two, but also of the persistence of forms of thinking and cultural expression that link these places together insofar as they distinguish themselves from the West. These forms of thinking are ultimately utilised in the film as a way of critiquing Western ideologies, in particular the metaphysics of "presence" in Western thought, its privileging of what is spoken to what is left unsaid.[38] In reflecting upon classical Japanese prose, which has comparatively few adverbs and adjectives, the cameraman remarks upon the lack of anthropomorphism in the Japanese language.[39] Here connotation discreetly inhabits the act of denoting without disrupting the concrete nature of language:

> To us, a sun is not quite a sun unless it's radiant, and a spring not quite a spring, unless it is limpid. Here to place adjectives would be so rude as leaving price tags on purchases. Japanese poetry never modifies. There's a way of saying, boat, rock, mist, frog, crow, hail, heron, chrysanthemum, that includes them all.[40]

For the cameraman, the journey between Africa and Japan is ultimately therefore "not a search for contrasts". Indeed, the observations and rapid intercuts between Africa and Japan are often suggestive of comparisons – pairing, for instance, the carnivals in Tokyo and Guinea-Bissau, or the nomadic people of the Cape Verde coastline, and the drifting populations of the Tokyo homeless, or the

African coastline and the Shiba coastline. It is in these "two extreme poles of survival" that the cameraman notes the persistence of a form of "animism" – a belief that "every fragment of creation has its invisible counterpart" and a use of animals as "mediators" of human sensibility.[41] In the course of the film, the examination of the various dimensions of this animism shifts from being a central component of the commentary's preoccupations and imagery (i.e. in the footage of the temple consecrated to cats; the statues and sculptures depicting animals; the constant imagery of animals interspersed throughout the film) to being subtly enfolded within the film's own discourse, the commentary eventually taking on the idiom of this "Japanese animism".

If the journey through the everyday life of Japan and Africa is, on one level, a very material and specific exploration of the contemporary landscape, the journey of *Sunless* also becomes a passage through to the past, an interior journey. The cameraman is persistently drawn back to reflections from his past, and most saliently to the violent political clashes and revolutionary culture of the 1960s, looking back to this era both to assess its failure to bring about the political changes sought, and to redefine the present political climate. Footage from the political struggles of the 1960s, including images of guerrilla warfare, public protests, social conflicts and struggles for independence, is constantly intercut with images from the present. In one respect, Marker's aim here is to map out the discontinuities between the political landscape of the 1960s and that which prevails today. Yet, Marker's aim is not only to gauge the gulf between two political cultures, but also to trace the subtle ties that bind the present to the past, to show how the burden of the political "fallout" of the 1960s continues to determine the present.

In *Sunless*, the everyday is everywhere inhabited by the traces of the past. In the opening sequences, we are immediately made aware of the way in which the banal and the incidental can trigger associations of previous times, or even imaginings of future times. Onboard the ferry from Hokkaido, we are shown images of commuters from the island, reading the papers, absorbed in reflection or ennui, or simply snatching moments of sleep as they are delivered across the shore. Yet, these humdrum images are the spur for the filmmaker's recollections of the wars he experienced during the 1960s. The pensive moments of reflectiveness and irritation amongst the commuters and, above all, the sleeping bodies slumped across the ferry's chairs are framed by the camera, soundtrack and commentary in such a way as to resemble the captives or victims of "a past or future war". Figures swathed in blankets appear as if they were corpses; fragments of limbs seen from close range look like the human remains of a battle; and the ferry itself comes to resemble a "fallout shelter". The tableaux in sum present an evocation of the way "small fragments of war" become "enshrined in everyday life" – encoded all the more resonantly in that the "discreet contents" of the banal offer an almost blank canvas for memory to imprint itself upon.

The filmmaker's long-standing ambivalence about the political culture of the 1960s and its aftermath forms a leitmotif of the film, a constant reference point in his reflections on the present, past and future. On the one hand, the cameraman expresses a certain exasperation with the naïvety of the ideals of this era for achieving its social vision of the future, pointing to the ideological faultlines in its thinking – in particular, its utopian uniting, in a common cause, of the dispossessed and those rebelling against their own privilege. Indeed, as he sardonically comments, many of the militants "studied capitalism so thoroughly to fight it that they now provide it with its best executives".[42] Yet, on the other hand, there is genuine admiration for the sense of outrage and collective ideals that impelled a generation to revolt, and a nostalgia for the sentiments encapsulated in Che Guevara's statement, "I tremble with indignation every time an injustice is committed in the world". The desire to change the order of things in the 1960s led student movements to take to the streets in protest against imperialist interventions in South Vietnam and Czechoslovakia and neo-colonialism in Chile, and to support the cause of freedom fighters in the wars of independence across the "Third World". Moreover, as Marker eloquently observes, if the ideals that had driven the protesters onto the streets had concretely failed, nevertheless "all they had won in their understanding of the world could have been won only through the struggle".

The film is pervaded, therefore, by a melancholy reflection on the failure of the radicalism of the 1960s to achieve its common aims, the persistence of the "same old struggles" that seemed once to be drawing to a close. During his return to Tokyo's Narita Airport to attend the anniversary commemorating a victim who had died during the civil protests against its construction, the cameraman is perplexed to discover, ten years later, the same protests still continuing, but now in the form, as he puts it, of a "shattered hologram" of the 1960s' generation. This sequence points not only to the failure of the original struggle, but also to the futility of the ongoing struggle whose cause is already lost. Such gestures, as he implies, consign revolutionary culture to the realm of empty rituals, which merely serve to "recycle" and display the formalised "signs" of struggle and the "postures" of revolutionary revolt and resistance.[43]

Aware of the tendency of the Left to drift from specific concrete initiatives to abstract mythologising, Marker draws out the divisions between "revolutionary romanticism" and the pragmatic issues of post-revolutionary struggle; "to work, to produce, to distribute, to overcome postwar exhaustion, temptations of power and privilege". Included within the former is the very notion of "guerrilla filmmaking" itself, which too often, Marker suggests, treated the recording of revolutionary campaigns as "an adventure". Indeed, the very term he states was "shamefully inappropriate" when compared to the suffering endured by the combatants. As so often is the case, militant filmmaking was misled by appearances.[44] Believing itself to be filming the overthrow of imperialism and the end of the age of the bourgeoisie, it was merely recording history's appearances.

The focal point of his treatment of this issue is the bitter ironies of the aftermath of the revolutionary struggle of Guinea-Bissau and the Cape Verde islands to free themselves from Portuguese colonialism. Marker frequently returns to this event as a watershed moment, for it was a war that galvanised the Left and temporarily inspired the hope of a new revolution in Europe. In the course of the film, we retrace the steps by which the revolution ultimately ended in a military coup. This unfolds in the form of a revisitation to the key sites of the war's history. The cameraman returns to the Fogo bay where the events began that led to the insurgence in 1959. He also returns to the river that borders the Bijago in Guinea-Bissau, a revisitation whose footage is poignantly intercut with archive film of Amilcar Cabral, the soon-to-be-assassinated revolutionary leader of the Partido Africano da Independência da Guiné e Cabo Verde (PAIGC; African Party for the Independence of Portuguese Guiné and Cape Verde), waving a parting gesture to the shore that he will never see again. This footage is, in turn, intercut with that of Louis Cabral, his half-brother, who was to become president of the newly-formed independent nation of Guinea, making the same gesture along the same river. Marker then cuts from images, taken during the war, of the soldiers embracing in an act of comradeship and solidarity, to footage in 1980 of a military award ceremony that shows Louis Cabral decorating and embracing Major Nino. The camera captures the distraught figure of Nino, who seems overcome by the event. Yet, as the commentary reveals, behind this ceremony commemorating the brotherhood of the struggle: "There lay a pit of post-victory bitterness and that Nino's tears did not express an ex-warrior's emotion, but the wounded pride of a hero who felt he had not been raised high enough above the others." One year later, a military coup will ensue, Cabral will be imprisoned, the PAIGC will have split, Guineans and Cape Verdeans will be divided again, and Nino will have come to power.

We gradually recognise that these passages dealing with the war of independence in Guinea stand for much more than the particular events they describe. For, at the heart of Marker's reflection upon the events of the 1960s is the retracing of the splintering and loss of direction of radical left-wing thought during this period, a capitulation that provokes a melancholic fatalist vision of the "advancement" of history. This fatalism which permeates the general tone of the film is most memorably incarnated at the conclusion of the discussion of the failure of the independence movement in Guinea. Having concluded his analysis of the events that led to the military coup, the commentary remarks:

> That's the way the breakers recede and so predictably that one has to believe in a kind of amnesia of the future that History distributes through mercy or calculation to those whom it recruits. Amilcar murdered by members of his own party, the liberated areas fallen under the yolk of bloody, petty tyrants, liquidated in their turn by a central power, to whose stability everyone paid homage until the military coup. That's how History advances, plugging its memory as one plugs one's ears. Louis exiled to Cuba. Nino discovering in his turn plots woven against him, can be cited reciprocally to appear before the bar of History. She doesn't care. She understands nothing. She has only one friend, the one Brando spoke of in 'Apocalypse'...Horror, that has a name and a face.

In the light of this, the viewer, aware of the cameraman's involvement in the struggles, whose revolutionary conflicts and militant confrontations had formed the subject-matter of many of his previous films, cannot but read his weariness with everything except banality in a new light, as the intellectual and emotional counterpart of the "post-68" political watershed. Travelling through time and space in *Sunless*, Marker maps out for us a trajectory which reveals the gradual diminishing of expectations for leftist intellectuals of his generation. The memory of time and place is permeated by a certain dolour, captured most poignantly in the words of the poet Samura Koichi, quoted in *Sunless*:

> Who said that time heals all wounds? It would be better to say that time heals everything except wounds. With time, the hurt of separation loses its real limits. With time, the desired body will soon disappear, and if the desiring body has already ceased to exist for the other, then what remains is a wound disembodied.

## Representation, reflexivity and history

Since the 1950s, self-reflexivity has been a defining characteristic of Marker's cinema. However, *Sunless* is one of the most self-conscious and intricately composed of Marker's films, constantly referring to its own processes of construction, and examining the nature of different forms of representation.[45] This self-reflexivity is an indispensable aspect of the structure of the film and the advancement of its main themes. Like many on the Left, Marker has wanted his work to represent a model of counter-cinema, and those aspirations have centred on the deployment of techniques that interrogate the conventions of cinema.[46] Following in the tradition of Brecht, Marker has fostered conventions of estrangement, intransitivity, non-closure, and the foregrounding of representational conventions in order that the viewer should constantly be aware of the constructing operations that are at play within film, and adopt a critically reflective attitude towards both what is represented and the way in which it is represented.[47]

For Marker, it is an ethical imperative of representation that it declare its means, rather than present film as a transitive instrument of reality. In this respect, Marker's critical use of self-reflexivity as a technique of raising self-consciousness should be differentiated from the more conservative and modish uses of self-reflexivity in much contemporary postmodernism.[48] Devices for keeping the framing operations of the cinematic medium at the forefront of our consciousness comprise, on the one hand, strategies of interruption which draw the viewer's attention to the processes of construction, such as altering the speed of the film, freezing an image, substituting photographs for moving footage, or "tampering" with the image – for instance, "arbitrarily" altering the colour tones of images and sequences.[49] This self-reflexivity extends even to discussing openly the processes of composition. Throughout the film, there is a constant stream of questions being posed about how to film, how to edit, how to convey the feelings associated with a particular moment or image. These reflexive observations are intricately intertwined with metacommentaries on film as a medium and reflections upon the nature of representation *per se*. These forms of self-consciousness, as in the above, take a number of forms, but share a consistent complication of the perspective through which we view the film. In the most straightforward of these, Marker, as mentioned already, at several points invokes the long-standing metaphor of the passage of a train as a symbol for the processes of "conveyance" within the cinematic medium itself.[50] In the first of these examples, a metropolitan train, with its long succession of carriages, is tracked by a static, centrally-placed camera as it travels the entire length from one side of the screen to the other, alluding thereby to the succession of filmic frames passing before an immobile spectator.[51] This metaphor is further augmented later on, as we are shown the inside of a train carriage, by the implied parallel between the immobility, anticipation and dreamlike state of the passengers in the train and the subject position of the cinematic spectator.[52]

Other sequences, on the other hand, provide a more convoluted form of reflexivity that problematises the very identity and status of the film itself. *Sunless* opens, for instance, with the enunciator referring to a future project of the cameraman, a project in which he would gather together images that had a special personal significance for him. As the enunciator speaks, some of the images of this "future" project begin to appear on the screen and the title, "*Sans soleil/Sunless*", appears. Towards the end of the film, this "future" project is rearticulated. Dwelling on the nature of memory, the cameraman hesitantly invents a "sketch" for a science-fiction film. As this segment draws to a close, the voice-over ironically comments:

> Of course I'll never make that film. Nonetheless, I'm collecting the sets, inventing the twists, putting in my favourite creatures. I've even given it a title, indeed the title of those Mussorgsky songs: 'Sunless'.

Such ambiguous passages may be taken to imply that the film is in the process of being composed, rather than completed, thus complicating the temporal dimension of the film and refusing the notion of closure. Indeed, Marker seems to intimate that *Sunless*'s existence is itself contingent, that the film could be reconstituted in different forms and that the finished project represents only one manifestation in time of the original project. Alternatively, it may be taken as a device to place the film *sous rature* (under erasure).[53] In each respect, it is the indeterminacy of the film's status that matters.

There are also passages, such as the Tokyo subway sequence referred to earlier, that critically examine the intricacies of the relationship of representational media to material reality, questioning the way in which our perception of the world is saturated by different forms of representational media. Indeed, *Sunless* constantly shifts between different levels of representation and different levels of reality, analysing the mediating role of representational media in our collective histories and personal memories. In the course of the film, we are exposed to various forms of film footage, digitalised imagery, televisual images, animated cartoons, video games, prints, sculpture, photographs, advertising billboards and taped sound: it is out of this heteroglossia that the filmmaker's memories are in part reconstituted. The referential status of these memories, however, is persistently questioned. Towards the end of the film, the enunciator, reading from the filmmaker's letters, remarks:

> Brooding at the end of the world...I remembered that month of January in Tokyo, or rather I remember the images I filmed of the month of January in Tokyo. They have substituted themselves for my memory, they are my memory.

As this quotation suggests, Marker's concern here turns on two interrelated axes. On the one hand, Marker insists on there being no simple equivalence between the photographic images that record an event and events themselves, undermining any notion of an immanent relation between the two.[54] As in Stendhal's *La Vie de Henri Brulard* (1890), where the narrator recalling the scene of a battle in which he was once engaged becomes aware that what he is describing is not the battle, but his recollection of an engraving made of it, the cameraman is constantly aware of the lacunae between representation and events.[55] On the other hand, the fact that the photographic image possesses the capacity to outlive the actual event it depicts complicates our ability to discriminate between what occurred and our representations of it. Indeed, the photographic image as a trace of an event acquires a materiality that substitutes itself for the contingency of the passing moment it depicts. Complicating this still further, any attempt to preserve a simple opposition between events and the images used to depict them has to take into account the presence of technologies such as film or photography at those events. This presence represents an intervention, one that inflects and shapes the experiences and events it seeks to record. This is most explicit in the sequences in the Cape Verde islands, where Marker draws attention to the, by turn overt and covert attitudes adopted by the islanders he is seeking to film to their knowledge of the camera's presence.[56]

Yet, if, in *Sunless*, Marker implies that new technologies of imaging have relativised the perception of the past to the point where reality is "overlaid" by representation, this argument does not, however, deny the existence of realities that exceed the means of representation by which we depict the events, but rather points to the image as a site not of plenitude, but of loss. It is precisely to this issue of the "semantic gaps" between the experiences of events and the representations by which we recall them that Marker continually returns. In one sequence, for instance, dwelling on the way in which certain material experiences remain impermeable to memory and inexpressible in representation, the film comes to an abrupt halt, frozen on an image of an African woman being transported across the sea in a rowing boat. Just before this point, the commentary states: "How can one remember thirst?". Likewise, Marker frequently draws our attention to what does not appear in the image, but was there in the experience of filming an event, and, contrariwise, what appears in the footage but had gone unnoticed in the filming of the event.

It is on account of this lack of an immanent relationship between representation and events that Marker employs strategies of "non-representation", regularly calling into question and even undermining the status of what is shown and what is said, by using techniques that "rupture" the codes of representational systems or induce semantic indeterminacy. One of the ways in which this is achieved is through the dialectical contestation of languages. Earlier, I mentioned the way in which Marker strategically uses some of the idioms and conventions of Japanese language and myth as a way of critiquing fundamental concepts inherent in Western thought. In turn, these reflections become critically engaged with the question of imaging, most explicitly in the aforementioned sequence that juxtaposes an analysis of Japanese television with Yamaneko's video images.

After scanning late-night television, the commentary turns our attention to Yamaneko's machine, the "zone", an overt reference to Tarkovskij's *Stalker* (1979), in which images of – among other things – student protest clashes from the 1960s, extracts of Kurosawa Akira's *Shichinin no samurai* (*Seven Samurai*, 1954) and documentary footage of the Kamikaze sorties off the coast of Okinawa during the Second World War are transformed by synthesiser technology. Faced by the exasperating endurance of forms of political oppression and the disparity between the appearance of change and the persistence of the same old struggles recurring time and again throughout history, Yamaneko's machine is presented as providing a certain "solution": "If the images of the present don't change, then change the images of the past".

From a cellar in Tokyo, Yamaneko responds to the dilemmas of cultural memory and the contingencies of history by "attacking", with the zeal of a "fanatic", images stored in the computer's memory, "taking them apart" in his machine.[57] Fed into the "Zone", fragments of images of the past are "de-realised", translated into images proper that no longer have entirely legible form. Yamaneko uses the machine to create an archive of personally composed "legends" stripped of their context and temporality. Out of this space a parallel world of images emerges, a world transmuted by thought, one which represents the indexical image in terms of a pageant of flowing plural energies and fragmentary intensities of colour and shape.

As we see the procession of these synthesised images, the commentary draws a distinction between the characteristic "realist" forms of presenting contemporary and historical events on television, and the "zone's" transfigurations, commenting that these images lie less "than those you see on television. At least they proclaim themselves to be what they are: images, not the portable and compact form of an already inaccessible reality".[58]

The "memory box" of the television, with its crush of "alienated" images, characteristically occludes the signs of its manufacture, reasserting the fit between representation and the world, and all the while imparting ideological messages below the threshold of consciousness. The "Zone", by contrast, takes cultural memory as its subject-matter, but only to transform those representations into an ever-mutable and opaque surface.

Extending this critique of representation beyond its context in the film, some interpreters have regarded this redemptive aspect of Yamaneko's strategies of imaging as indicative of Marker's own sceptical flight from political engagement into the abstractions of imaging in and for itself. Yet, we should be wary of such simple equations, since the persistence in Marker's work of themes of political injustice argues against this view.[59] It is rather in the ideological contestation of systems of imaging that the "zone" has meaning. The "zone" is not therefore an ultimate "answer" to the dilemma of representation and history, but one contingent procedure that may, at strategic intervals, be deployed to induce a critical consciousness of that dilemma. Hence, although Marker uses the palette of the "zone's" prism, this is not at the expense of other forms of imaging, but rather within the interplay of alternative "languages" of imaging.

Moreover, if "the zone" eschews representation or, more particularly, the immanent relation of the image to the events it "records", it does not relinquish the role of signification. Instead, it becomes the vehicle both for expressing the limits of representation, and for alluding to a reality that exceeds visible appearances. Replaying through the "zone" footage of the Tokyo beggars seen earlier ("Men...whose names are taboo") the voice-over comments: "They are non-persons, how can they be shown, except as non-images". Equally, in another sequence, the commentary reads the ambivalent thoughts contained in a letter from a Kamikaze pilot, while images of the ceremonies before their flight and the shooting down of the pilots attacking US battleships are fed through the Zone's "prism". The letter, with its poignant meditations on the situation of the Kamikaze, exposes a hidden history of the coercion of the pilots, who, torn between the long-standing codes of military honour and patriotism, derived as Marker shows from the traditions of the Sumari, and their consciousness of the futility of this self-sacrifice, could see no way out. The transfigured appearance of the images serves as a metaphor for the estrangement from conventional history that these letters provide. They place this footage "under erasure" in a comparable manner to the way in which the letters compromise the Japanese "official history" of the Kamikaze.

Ultimately, therefore, the question of reflexivity is inseparable from the larger issue of representation as a function of memory. This is also true in respect of the intricate *mise en abîme* and intertextual references that are scattered throughout the film. As this interpretation of *Sunless* has progressed, it has become clear that Marker's film constructs a series of dialogues with other "texts" – Sei Shōnagon's *The Pillow Book*, for example, or Mussorgsky's "Sunless". Besides these, Marker establishes transtextual relationships to a number of films, through either direct quotation or allusion. Some of these make reference to films of directors he admires or with whom he has collaborated. There are sequences and voice-overs that refer to, or quote from, among others, Tarkovskij's *Stalker*, Kurosawa Akira's *Seven Samurai*, Cocteau's *Le Sang d'un poète* (*The Blood of a Poet*, 1930), Godard's *Weekend* (1967), Tati's *Playtime* (1967), Coppola's *Apocalypse Now* and Hitchcock's mesmerising *Vertigo*, a film to which Marker has constantly made recourse, most especially in *La Jetée*. Moreover, in the sequence which immediately follows the titles, Marker evokes the opening to Dziga Vertov's *Čelovek s kinoapparaton* (*The Man with a Movie Camera*, 1929) by following a group of citizens from pre-dawn to awakening.

Other intertextual sequences of the film refer to Marker's own work. The opening recalls *Letter from Siberia*, and references and allusions to his previous films abound in *Sunless*. The most notable of these are to *La Jetée*, a film which is also a reflection on time, travel, memory, history and cinema. Like *La Jetée*, *Sunless* allusively opens with an image of childhood and planes that is replaced with those of death and apocalypse. The visit in *Sunless* to the Japanese "sex chapel" which displays in glass cases specimens of preserved animals posed in acts of copulation recalls the visit made to the natural history museum in *La Jetée*, a scene that in the latter stands for the preservation of time. The Tokyo subway sequence also evokes the subterranean tunnels that provide the setting of *La Jetée*. As this suggests, intertextual references within the film evoke memories and augment lines of thought in the film. For instance, the wire and wool "mobile" of a muse's head hanging from the ceiling of Yamaneko's studio, a borrowing from Cocteau's *The Blood of a Poet*, associates the "zone" with the world of Cocteau's film, an irrational world reformulated according to the logic of the imagination. Indeed, in the extraordinary scene that follows the appearance of the muse's head, the studio becomes animated and artificially illuminated in a way that recalls the magical incarnations of Cocteau's film.

The most important and complex of these intertexts refers to Hitchcock's *Vertigo*, in a sequence that provides a re-creation and reading of this intricate detective story. In *Vertigo*, Hitchcock's detective Scottie is hired to follow and report on Madelene, the wife of an old friend, who believes she is possessed by the spirit of Carlotta Valdes, who committed suicide after a tragic love affair many years before Madelene's birth. As the plot gradually unfolds, Scottie's ability to unravel the tangled web of illusions and events becomes more and more tenuous, and appearances are not what they seem to be. Eventually, by a strange twist of fate, he will find himself unwittingly complicit in "Madelene's death" on two occasions.

The film's re-enactment of Scottie's trail is not only a cinematographic, but also a psychological, journey that both parallels the structural path of *Sunless* and retranslates Hitchcock's film into Marker's own idiom. Marker uses photographic stills from *Vertigo* intercut with his own film footage, to retrace Scottie and Madelene's footsteps. This amounts to a tour of the routes and sites of *Vertigo*, but Marker also reconstructs, with subtle differences, some of the scenes, which are edited as if to approximate the semblance of memory. Marker uses the narrative of *Vertigo* not only to illustrate the workings of memory, but also to have his representation of *Vertigo* as a demonstration of the complex interlinking of past and present. This is evident in the way in which he transforms *Vertigo* by conflating it with the memory of his own films. Those familiar with Marker's previous work will already know how *Vertigo* provided the structure for the plots of *Le Mystère Koumiko* (1965) and *La Jetée*, the latter of which is told, with the exception of one brief moment, exclusively through the juxtaposition of photo-stills. In *Sunless*, the scene in *La Jetée* which reworks the moment in *Vertigo* – when Madelene implausibly points out to Scottie a place within the concentric circles of the sequoia tree from where she has come and to where she belongs – is obliquely inserted into the retracing of *Vertigo's* narrative. Moreover, this re-creation of *Vertigo* is achieved by translating

Hitchcock's film into the idiom of *La Jetée*'s photo-stills.

The *Vertigo* sequence is memorably used by Marker in *Sunless* to recapitulate and develop further issues about power and freedom, and time and history. For Marker, *Vertigo* is more than an obsessive love story; rather, it offers a sceptical meditation on the nature of history. It is the only film, so the commentary states, to have adequately presented "impossible memory, insane memory", and a film that has acquired a particular obsession for the "filmmaker" who, it is stated, has seen it nineteen times. In examining the intricacies of *Vertigo*'s plot, a complex *mise en abîme* is elaborated, in which, like a play of mirrors within mirrors, *Vertigo* acts as a commentary on *Sunless* and vice versa.

Marker provides in this sequence both a re-enactment of the narrative of *Vertigo* and, at the same time, an allegorical reading of the film, characterising Scottie as "Time's Fool of Love". Beneath the surface of the plot lies a subtle commentary on the nature of time and memory:

> In the spiral of the titles he saw time covering a field ever wider as it moved away, a cyclone whose present moment contains motionless; the eye. In San Francisco he had made his pilgrimage to all the film's locations. The florist...where James Stewart spies on Kim Novak, he the hunter, she the prey, or was it the other way around...He had driven up and down the hills of San Francisco where Jimmy Stewart's Scottie follows Kim Novak/Madelene. It seems to be a question of trailing, of enigma, of murder, but in truth it's a question of power and freedom, of melancholy and dazzlement, so carefully coded within the spiral that you could miss it, and not discover immediately that this vertigo of space in reality stands for the vertigo of time.

Marker reveals that the protagonists' relations, and thus the relations of power, are not only liable to change, but also subject to misrecognition. Hitchcock's "all-seeing" detective is, in reality, blind to the actual course of events, and, at the point when he finally feels that he has mastered the situation, he will ironically be helpless to prevent the repetition of Madelene's death. At each stage in the narrative, Scottie will unknowingly be the catalyst through which events unfold, events which are ultimately beyond his control. The passage reconstructing *Vertigo* is, as the above quotation indicates, dominated by the motif of the spiral, "the spiral of time", which, in the original film, recurs as a leitmotif at various intervals: in the opening credits; in the spirals of the concentric circles of the sequoia tree; in the coiffure of the portrait of the dead Carlotta; and in the coiffure of Madelene herself, and which, in *Sunless*, adorns the hair of the mobile of the muse in the "zone". This motif represents for Marker a metaphor for the "labyrinth of history", one that invokes two sources. The first of these is Hegel's use of the spiral in his "Logic" as a metaphor for the progression of History and the way in which notions recur in history in a constantly developing form. The implications of Hegel's metaphor are that the objects of consciousness do not remain stable, but are continually reshaped in the light of changes in consciousness, a notion that has rightly led him to be seen as the pre-eminent philosopher of the temporal. Yet, for Hegel, the temporal is ultimately conceived teleologically as a forward progression towards the transcendence of History itself, whilst, for Marker, the figure of the spiral presents a view of history as in a continual state of becoming whose unfolding can never be completed.

Indeed, Marker's ideas about history, although critically engaged with Hegel, are in certain respects more closely aligned to Nietzsche, for, through the metaphor of the spiral, Marker also alludes to Nietzsche's idea of the eternal return. The notion of the eternal return presents us with a paradox: history implies change and development, but, looking at history over the long term, it may be perceived that certain patterns of events seem to recur regularly. Yet, is this recurrence actual or merely an effect of perspective? Nietzsche's paradox of the eternal return implies that what returns will never actually return as the same, but will only be "recognised" as "the same" by virtue of its temporal difference. What recurs returns in the form of a misrecognition, for it is only what the present recognises of itself in the past, not the past in itself. But this trick of perspective has real effects in the present, for it is on the basis of this misrecognition of the past that perceptions and actions in the present are founded. Therefore, ironically, it is the perception of the eternal return that perpetuates the patterns of the past in the present.

The narrative thread of *Vertigo* may be read as presenting a discreet variation on this theme of the misrecognition of the past. Believing himself responsible for Madelene's death, Scottie, oblivious to his illusions and his misreading of events, obsessively revisits the sites of the past in an effort to redeem himself. He returns to the places where he had trailed Madelene, and even attempts to recuperate the past "as it was", by creating a "surrogate Madelene" to take the "dead Madelene's" place. In doing so, however, he creates in the present the conditions by which Madelene is finally lost to him. Deceived by the appearances of history, he is doomed to repeat the patterns of the past.

Subtly integrated into the very fabric of *Sunless*, the *Vertigo* sequence echoes what has gone before and what will follow. This is achieved firstly in the form of the allusion to the moment in *Vertigo* when Madelene points to the place in time from which she is supposed to have originated, a gesture which recurs in *La Jetée* and throughout *Sunless*, and secondly, through the correspondences which Marker sets up between the *Vertigo* sequence and actual historical events and fictional sequences occurring earlier and later in *Sunless*. In the first instance, the image of an outstretched hand pointing to a place somewhere in time is ubiquitously linked in the film with an array of other images of outstretched arms. The gesture recurs, among other instances, in the posters of Pope John Paul II; in the obscure rituals of a strange "alien tribe" of street dancers, and in the kimonoed dancers during a carnival in Tokyo; in the sequence in which travellers board the subway; in the gestures of the colonial statues and demonstrating protesters; and even in the gesture of the saluting votive figurines of cats. Most poignantly, however, it recurs in the aforementioned gesture of the doomed Amilcar Cabral, waving farewell from the shoreline, in the acquired footage of the war of independence in Guinea-Bissau.

In the second instance, the underlying theme of the revisitation of the past in the retracing of Scottie's footsteps recalls various earlier and later sequences in which the cameraman returns to places that are deeply engrained in his memory. At the beginning, we retrace the cameraman's return to Tokyo and his revisiting of once-familiar sites. Later, we also follow him on his return to the Cape Verde islands, where he surveys the aftermath of the postwar landscape for the signs of the continued struggle for independence, and, later still, to a village where he once stayed in Iceland. In each instance, we are taken on a tour of the familiar landmarks which once provided the orienting points of his journeys, but, as with the reconstruction of the sites of *Vertigo*, these journeys are marked by loss and rupture, for, although the majority of the sites have remained, some have vanished, and those that have persisted no longer exist in the same form. The village in Iceland, for example, has been partially destroyed by a volcanic eruption.

The *Vertigo* sequence is further interlinked with a segment towards the end of the film, where the commentary dwells on the aforementioned "abortive" sketch for a film to be entitled *Sunless*. At this point, the commentary returns full circle to the opening image of children in Iceland. The narrator then elaborates further on the nature of the intended project. Like *La Jetée*, this was to be a science-fiction film, but, set on the wasted landscape of another planet or, alternatively, on our own planet. The protagonist in this story is a man "who has forgotten how to forget". He is an "alien" who comes from the future from the year 4001. In this future, the human brain has been perfected, and people have total recall. From where he comes, there is no alienated image; to call forth an image or a memory is to be aware of the origins of the "long and painful pre-history" from which it has arisen, and yet something vital still eludes. The visitor has been drawn to this terrain by his wish to understand Mussorgsky's song cycle "Sunless", still sung in the 40th century, and it is through his attempt to come to terms with this piece of music that he dimly "perceived the presence of that thing he didn't understand", the relationship between "unhappiness and memory".

Paradoxically, the experience of forgetting, the gaps in our recollection of the past, is seen not to be the antithesis of memory, but commensurate with memory and the advancement of history. As the enunciator reading from the letters of the cameraman states:

> I will have spent my life trying to understand the function of remembering, which is not the opposite of forgetting, but rather its lining. We do not remember, we rewrite memory much as history is rewritten.

Total recall is, in effect, total anaesthesia, and the archivist utopia of memory perfected is revealed to be the very opposite of living memory and hence of a living culture. Devoid of this living history, the beings of 4001 are condemned eternally to rerun the past in its entirety "in order to know it existed".

Conclusion

Gradually, in the course of *Sunless*, Marker unfolds an intricate meditation on the writing and rewriting of history, and it is only by understanding the arguments Marker puts forward about history that one grasps the underlying intellectual structure of the film. In Marker's work – and *Sunless* is no exception – we are conscious that the history which he presents does not draw us into the illusion of transparency, as if the past were simply there, present, intact, waiting for us. With Marker we are always aware that history, like memory, is, to paraphrase the historian Michel de Certeau, a treatment for absence.[60] This absence remains at the centre of history, for what is represented of the past is merely a series of fragments. Detached from the midst of its material environment, these fragments can never be wholly reconstituted. Correspondingly, the representation of history is neither commensurate with the events it represents, nor equivalent to the experience of those who have participated in those events. The lack of common measure that inevitably exists between the views of historical events as "official versions of collective memory" and the scale of personal experience detaches history from its source in material perception and consciousness. For the individual experiencing historical events, history remains recalcitrantly "invisible", for it is the event, not the causality, that is experienced.

Rejecting the idea of history as simply a "mirror" of events, Marker implies instead that the writing of history does not simply record or reproduce events as they were, but gives form to, and perpetually transforms, those events. Our understanding of the past is therefore only the sum total of representations that can be made of it at any one moment in time. Yet, the problem is deeper than a self-conscious recognition of the limits of historical recuperation. For the problem of historical interpretation is also bound up with the experience of temporality. History is caught in a double bind; if what the present understands about the past is never simply the past as it was, it is equally true that our understanding of the present is always refracted through our imperfect recollection of the past. This implies that past and present are ultimately inseparable, for the present continually inhabits our perception of the past, and the past our perception of the present. We are ultimately unable to disentangle what we project back onto the past from the past itself, for we are incapable of detaching ourselves fully from the present. Our inability to stand "outside of history" means that we are ill-equipped to judge whether there is an underlying order to the apparent randomness and chaos of historical events, because the order of history – if, indeed, it exists – must exist beyond the limits of our perception, and thus beyond the reach of our understanding. The problems of history thus become enmeshed in a series of problems of perspective. The fact that the observation of history is made from a vantage point within history relativises the knowledge it seeks to provide of the world, and thus undermines its claims to objective neutrality or secure foundations.

In the course of *Sunless*, Marker draws our attention to these problems of the writing of history, adopting a radical scepticism about the limits of historical representation, the attendant blindness and misrecognition that accompany our attempts to stand apart from and grasp the unfolding of historical process. At one point questioning the forces which are determining the power relations of the modern global economy, the commentary states: "Do we ever know where history is really made?". More poignantly, the frequent exposition of moments of interpretive "blindness" counters the persistent imagery of the omniscient eye that runs throughout the film. Indeed, as we have recognised at times in *Sunless*, there is a personification of history, as a mythical figure, a muse of chaos, intransigent to the plight of the suffering, and wreaking havoc on the best-laid plans. This melancholy fatalism in *Sunless* implies that man does not make history, but endures it, or, put another way, that the unfolding of historical events always outstrips the interpretive frameworks which we bring to bear upon them.[61] In a satirical ode to the video game "Pacman", the commentary remarks that the game is:

> [T]he most perfect graphic metaphor of man's fate. He puts into true perspective the balance of power between the individual and the environment, and he tells us soberly that, though there may be honour in carrying out the greatest number of victorious attacks, it always comes a cropper.

In another sequence, preceding the discussion of the war of independence in Guinea, Marker, drawing on the use of animals as "mediators" in Japanese and African myth, uses the footage of the violent slaying of the giraffe as a metaphor for the vanquishing of the radical revolutionary forces of the 1960s. The destructive forces of time in their various cultural and natural manifestations are ever-present within the film, and even prevail upon the images of *Sunless* itself. Towards the conclusion of the film, the sequences of images that we have already seen in the course of the film are repeated, but now channelled through the distorted prism of the zone. The procession of recurring images filtered through Yamaneko's machine begins to take on a ritual destruction of the fragments of memory that the film has evoked. Indeed, at one point, an analogy is explicitly drawn between the effect of the filtering images on Yamaneko's machine and "letters which one burns, which are consumed at the edge of the fire". These words are accompanied by images of sacrifice, the burning of dolls, and the footage of Kamikaze planes in flames, processed through Yamaneko's machine.

Yet, if *Sunless* uses the language of myth to form a critique of the rational and humanist vision of history, this pessimism about the scope of history is not intended to negate history as a form of knowledge. *Sunless* is nothing if not the attempt to interpret history, to decipher what lies beneath the appearances of history and to recover what has been buried within the annals of history. Marker perpetually draws our attention to what may otherwise be forgotten. Recalling the war in Guinea, the commentary asks plaintively: "Who remembers all that? History throws its empty bottles out the window". Similarly, in the sequence of the visit to Okinawa, he laments the passing of the Ryoko, the native inhabitants of the island, whose population was devastated during the American invasion in 1945. *Sunless* therefore, in Marker's own words, attempts to "repair the web of time" where it has been broken.[62]

The problem of representing history for Marker is bound up with finding another way to write history, one that acknowledges, rather than occludes, the processes of constructing history; a form of history that finds a place for history's indeterminacies, in terms of both the limits of representation and the problems that beset our understanding of the temporal. That other way for Marker involves an attempt to convey something of "history's polyphony" and, through the mutability of signification and the refusal of closure, to represent history as a living presence. We might say that *Sunless* is a demonstration of such a model of history.[63]

Critical reception

*Sunless* was one of the few feature-length Marker films since the 1960s to appear in translation, and the first for some time to gain a relatively wide "art-house" distribution in Europe and the United States.[64] Hence, whilst in France, *Sunless* was discussed in the informed context of themes and issues of Marker's previous and most recent work, in Britain and the United States *Sunless* was largely greeted in the context of the return, after many years away from cinema, of the elusive filmmaker of such 1960s classics as *La Jetée*.

Although *Sunless* was generally acclaimed as a *"tour de force"* and the most important Marker film for many years, it predictably encountered some ambivalent, uncomprehending and even hostile reviews. These tended to come in short review format from film critics writing for the more populist film journals in Britain and the United States, who found the work obscure and the relation between commentary and image bewildering.[65] A further point of criticism was directed at the intricacies of Marker's montage. Derek Elley wrote:

> [A]ll too often the best of Marker's thoughts (and his images) fly past in the general melee...he has yet to master the peaks and troughs of feature length or learn the value of *multum in parvu*.[66]

Many of the more favourable longer reviews and articles concentrated on the "richness, complexity and allusiveness" of the film, analysing the manner of its "unfolding", and exploring the arguments about time and space in the film, and how they are woven into the theme of memory, history and representation.[67] Yet, the evident lack of access to much of Marker's output prevented a recognition of how the re-evocation of the memories of his previous films forms an integral part of this theme.

Those who compared *Sunless* to his previous documentary work were keen to stress a rupture between the film and works such as *Le Joli Mai* (1963), and to place this rather simplistically in the context of a gradual retreat by French filmmakers from political filmmaking. G D Van Cauwenberge wrote:

> Marker no longer strives in *Sans Soleil* toward confrontation in the name of ideological awareness as

was the aim of so many self-reflexive films in the 70s. Rather, he attempts to draw the viewer into the filmmaker's artistic choices, doubts, regrets, hesitations and, above all, his gratification derived from creating with images.[68]

Yet, for others, it was the continuity in Marker's work and the subtlety of Marker's film that impressed them. Chris Auty, in one of the more astute reviews, remarked:

> Marker's work remains uniquely approachable...While other political filmmakers of his generation shouted out positions like military drill, Marker has spent a quarter of a century devising eloquent haikus on the state of the world.[69]

These last words might form a fitting epigraph for the film.

## Notes

[1] Quoted in Eliane Perrin, "Sunless, or the living memory of Chris. Marker", *Scope Magazine* 1 (November 1992/January 1993): 22.

[2] The enunciator is Florence Delay in the French version, and Alexandra Stewart in the English version.

[3] Marker may have had in mind Chantal Akerman's *News from Home* (1976), where a similar strategy of narration is employed.

[4] On indeterminacy, see Wolfgang Iser, "Indeterminacy and the Reader's Response in Prose Fiction", in J Hillis Miller (ed), *Aspects of Narrative: Selected Papers from the English Institute* (New York; London: Columbia University Press, 1971): 1-45.

[5] See Anatole Dauman, "Chris Marker", in Jacques Gerber, *Souvenir-Ecran* (Paris: Centre Georges Pompidou, 1989): 149-151; G D Van Cauwenberge, *Chris Marker and French Documentary Filmmaking: 1962-1982* (PhD thesis, New York University, 1993): 216n4.

[6] In one instance, during a sequence reflecting on the underlying

significance of video games, the camera focuses on a player whilst the commentary discusses Yamaneko's "zone". Soon after we see shots of Yamaneko's studio and then return to the "player". The implication obviously suggests that we are meant to read this figure as Yamaneko, but Marker plainly leaves visible signs that make us conscious of the construction of this fictional identity. We are, for instance, aware that the private space of the studio is very different from the public space of the café where the video games are located with its commercial for Coca-Cola on the window. It is clear from the choice of shot and shot progression that the passage is supposed to be both a fictionalisation and the simultaneous undermining of that fictionalisation within one and the same sequence.

7    It is an increasingly characteristic trait of Marker's films that his films often refer to and incorporate material from his previous film to date, as well as making reference to his other works. Indeed, increasingly these films have an integral connection to each other.

8    Here Barthes' notion of a subject who engages in logical contradiction seems useful. See Roland Barthes, *The Pleasure of the Text*, translated by Richard Miller (Oxford, UK; Cambridge, USA: Blackwell, 1990): 3.

9    Van Cauwenberge: 217.

10   For a discussion of these ideas in relation to documentary film, see William Guynn, *A Cinema of Nonfiction* (Rutherford; Madison; Teaneck: Fairleigh Dickinson University Press; London; Toronto: Associated University Press, 1990): 159-160.

11   See Roland Barthes, "To Write an Intransitive Verb?", in Richard Macksey and Eugenio Donato (eds), *The Structuralist Controversy: The Languages of Criticism and the Sciences of Man* (Baltimore: The Johns Hopkins University Press, 1972): 134-145; Michael Holland (ed), *The Blanchot Reader* (London: Blackwell, 1996): 25-61, 143-156.

12   On the questioning of the fissuring of the notion of the self, see Chris Marker, *Le Dépays* (Paris: Herscher, 1982): n.p.

13   "[L]es lettres, les commentaires, les images recueillies, les images fabriquées, plus quelques images empruntées. Ainsi de ces

mémoires juxtaposées naît une mémoire fictive" ("The letters, the comments, the images gathered; the images created; together with some images borrowed. Out of these juxtaposed memories is born a fictional memory"). Excerpt from the *Sunless* press file in Gerber: 172. Marker's real name is Christian François Bouche-Villeneuve.

14    One exception to this is the film footage of Iceland after a volcanic eruption, which is acknowledged in the commentary as sent to him from Haroun Tazieff.

15    The choice of a single voice commentating also needs to be understood in the context of Marker's continual experimentation with narrating. In *Le Fond de l'air est rouge: Scènes de la troisième guerre mondiale 1967-77. Textes et description d'un film de Chris Marker* (1977), Marker had used seven different voices, male and female, many of them well-known, including François Maspero, Yves Montand, Simone Signoret and Marker himself, all notably persons of the same generation and associated with the Communist Party in the 1960s. Likewise, in *Level 5* (1997), he uses two, his own and that of the actress who plays the protagonist.

16    On autobiography, see H J Silverman, *Textualities: Between Hermeneutics and Deconstruction* (New York; London: Routledge, 1994): 89-135.

17    Marker has written of his editing processes in the following terms: "Editing, one would hope, restores history's polyphony. No place here for gratuitous linkages or mean spirited attempts at forcing people to contradict themselves (who hasn't contradicted himself at least once?)". Marker in respect of *Le Fond de l'air est rouge* also spoke of his desire through the negation of authoritarian commentary "to give back to the viewer his own commentary, his own power". See Marker (1977): 6-7.

18    Michael Walsh, "Around the World, Across All Frontiers: Sans Soleil as Dépays", *CineAction!* (autumn 1989): 32.

19    Ibid: 32-33.

20    As Walsh (32) points out, there is a discreet echo here of Marker's *Le Train en Marche* (*And the Train Rolls On*, 1973), his study of the Soviet filmmaker, Alexander Medvedkin.

21    A sequence in *Le Fond de l'air est rouge* clarifies the significance
      accorded to the original "flawed" footage. At one point in the film,
      a question flashes onscreen: "Why do images sometimes tremble?"
      This is immediately trailed with voice-over dialogue between
      filmmakers (including Marker's unidentified voice): "It happened
      to me in May 68 on Boulevard Saint-Michel". Another voice
      chimes in: "It happened to me in Prague during the summer of
      '68...when I saw the rushes. I saw the shaking image. Although
      I steadied my hands, the camera still seized the tremulous reality".
      Marker's remarks here about the power of reality to stamp its
      mark on the camerawork need to be distinguished from the use
      of unstable camerawork as a style.

22    Marker's strategies of presentation in this and in many other
      respects are closely aligned to the practices of the *nouveau roman*
      writers. See Alain Robbe-Grillet, *Snapshots and Towards a New
      Novel*, translated by Barbara Wright (London: Calder and Boyars,
      1965); Bruce Morrissette, *The Novels of Alain Robbe-Grillet* (Ithaca,
      New York: Cornell University Press, 1975): 21-38, 75-112. See
      also Maurice Merleau-Ponty, "Five Notes on Claude Simon", and
      "Merleau-Ponty Replies to Claude Simon 'Writer and Thinker'",
      in Celia Britton (ed), *Claude Simon* (London; New York:
      Longman, 1993): 35-38, 39-40, respectively.

23    See Julia Kristeva, *Powers of Horror: An Essay on Abjection*,
      translated by Leon S Roudiez (New York: Columbia University
      Press, 1982): 1-31.

24    Yvette Biro, "In the Spiral of Time", *Millennium Film Journal*
      (autumn/winter 1984/85): 174.

25    Ibid.

26    On Sei Shōnagon's writings, see André Beaujard, *Les Notes de
      chevet de Sei Shōnagon* (Paris: Gallimard, 1934); André Beaujard,
      *Sei Shōnagon: son temps et son œuvre* (Paris: Gallimard, 1934); and
      Ivan Morris, introduction to *The Pillow-Book of Sei Shōnagon*,
      translated by Arthur Waley (London: George Allen & Unwin,
      1928): 9-19.

27    See Gérard Genette, *Palimsestes: La litérature au Second degré*
      (Paris: Seuil, 1982); Gérard Genette, *Narrative Discourse*,
      translated by Jane E Lewin (Oxford: Basil Blackwell, 1980).

28    Translated from the French: "la façon d'une composition musicale, avec thèmes récurrents, contrepoints et fugues en miroir". Gerber: 172.

29    Joris Ivens, *The Camera and I* (Berlin: Seven Seas Publishers, 1969): 88.

30    *The Complete Poems and Plays of T S Eliot* (London: Faber and Faber, 1977): 89.

31    These include various landmarks including the Ginza owl on the front of a department store, the Shinbashi locomotive, and the Temple of the Fox at the top of the Mitsugushi department store. The commentary refers to the filmmaker's searching out of familiar sites as "like a cat who's come home from vacation in his basket immediately starts to inspect familiar places", and this is visually materialised in the suturing of viewpoint with images of cats' gazing across the city from rooftops and balconies.

32    On this metaphor of the city and music, see Andrew Bowie, "Music, Language and Modernity", in Andrew Benjamin (ed), *The Problems of Modernity* (London: Routledge, 1989): 67-85.

33    This way of attending to the city obviously has its source in the writings of Baudelaire and Simmel on 19th-century Paris. See Charles Baudelaire, *Œuvres Complètes* (Paris: Gallimard, 1961). Georg Simmel, *On Individuality and Social Forms: Selected Writings*, edited and with an introduction by Donald N Levine (Chicago; London: The University of Chicago Press, 1971). See also Victor Fournel, *Ce qu'on voit dans les rues de Paris* (Paris: Gallimard, 1858) and Walter Benjamin, *Charles Baudelaire: A Lyric Poet in the Era of High Capitalism*, translated by Harry Zohn (London: NLB, 1973).

34    Jean Baudrillard, "The Ecstasy of Communication", in Hal Foster (ed), *The Anti-Aesthetic: Essays on Postmodern Culture* (Seattle, Washington: Bay Press, 1983): 129.

35    See Michel Foucault, *Discipline and Punish: The Birth of the Prison*, translated by Alan Sheridan (London: Allen Lane, 1977): 26-30.

36    On the notion of spectacle, see Guy Debord, *La Société du Spectacle* (Paris: Buchet-Chastel, 1967). For its specific application to the study of the city, see T J Clark, *The Painting of Modern Life:*

*Paris in the Art of Manet and His Followers* (London: Thames and Hudson, 1985): 3-79.

37 There is a connection here to Baudrillard's notion of the "hyperreal". See Jean Baudrillard, *Simulations*, translated by Paul Foss, Paul Patton and Philip Beitchman (New York: Semiotext[e], 1983). See also Sadie Plant, *The Most Radical Gesture: The Situationist International in a postmodern age* (London; New York: Routledge, 1992): 5-6, 153-155.

38 On the critique of Western metaphysics, see Jacques Derrida, *Of Grammatology*, translated by Gayatri Chakravorty Spivak (Baltimore; London: The Johns Hopkins University Press, 1976).

39 On this critique of "anthropomorhic" language, see Robbe-Grillet: 75-96.

40 Indeed, Marker's own film might be compared to a haiku poem in that its evocativeness flows from a very compressed and concrete structure of allusive imagery.

41 "He wrote me that the Japanese secret, what Les Bistros have called the poignancy of things, implied the faculty of communing with things, of entering into them, of being them for a moment. It was normal that in their turn, they should be like us, perishable and immortal. He wrote me: animism is a familiar notion in Africa. It is less often applied in Japan. What then shall we call this diffuse belief according to which every fragment of creation has its invisible counterpart?".

42 On the decline of the hopes of the 1960s early in the subsequent decade, see Jean-Pierre Rioux, "Comment changer la vie?", in *Les idées en France 1945-1988: Une chronologie* (Paris: Gallimard, 1989): 290-292.

43 In a variation on this in *Le Fond de l'air est rouge*, Marker had intercut images of popular resistance and demonstration across the world with images from Eisenstein's *Bronenosets Potemkin* (*Battleship Potemkin*, 1925), suggesting, through graphic matching, the way in which apparently spontaneous gestures had themselves a formalised reference point in the representation of ideological struggle in film. See Van Cauwenberge: 209-210. See also Marker (1977): 180.

44   On militant filmmaking, see "Pour le dépérissement du cinéma militant", in "Table ronde sur 'Le fond de l'air est rouge' de Chris Marker", *Cahiers du Cinéma* 284 (January 1978): 46-51.

45   On the use of self-reflexive strategies within cinema, see Robert Stam, *Reflexivity in Film and Literature: From Don Quixote to Jean-Luc Godard* (Ann Arbor, MI: UMI Research Press, 1985).

46   A useful text for discussions of leftist counter-cinematic models is Jean-Louis Baudry, "Écriture/Fiction/Idéologie", *Tel Quel* 31 (autumn 1967): 15-30, translated by Daniel Matias in *Afterimage* 5 (spring 1974): 22-39.

47   On the revitalisation of the Brechtian tradition and the translation of Brecht's theories into a semiotic idiom, see, for example, Peter Wollen, *Signs and Meanings in the Cinema* (London: Secker and Warburg in association with the British Film Institute, 1972) and Peter Wollen, *Readings and Writings: Semiotic Counter-Strategies* (London: Verso, 1982).

48   See Jane Feuer, *The Hollywood Musical*, second edition (Bloomington; Indianapolis: Indiana University Press, 1993).

49   Here again we may detect the influence of the editing techniques of Soviet filmmakers such as Vertov and Eisenstein who used acceleration, deceleration, freeze-frame and reverse motion as ways of creating "anti-naturalist" temporal intervals. See Annette Michelson, "The Wings of Hypothesis: On Montage and the Theory of the Interval", in Matthew Teitelbaum (ed), *Montage and Modern Life 1919-1942* (Cambridge, MA; London: University of Michigan Press, 1993): 60-81; and Jon Kear, "Montage, modernity and its histories", *Word & Image* 11: 3 (July-September 1995): 320-326.

50   See Michelson: 60-82.

51   On the theorisation of the cinematic apparatus, see Christian Metz, "The Imaginary Signifier", *Screen* 16: 2 (summer 1975): 14-76. Walsh (32-33) has convincingly argued that the opening sequence, where images are separated by the intervention of black leader, is also an integral part of this metacommentary. This black leader, which acquires many associations as the film progresses, reflexively alludes to the condition of cinema itself.

52      Recognition of this metacommentary also reflects on the aforementioned opening sequence of travelling on the Hokkaido ferry, which again is also full of passengers waiting, immobile, snatching moments of sleep. See Christian Metz, *The Imaginary Signifier: Psychoanalysis and the Cinema*, translated by Celia Britton, Annwyl Williams, Ben Brewster and Alfred Guzzetti (Bloomington: Indiana University Press, 1982).

53      The strategy of placing concepts *sous rature* associated with the writings of Heidegger and later Derrida may be defined as the simultaneous invoking and questioning of a concept.

54      In *Si j'avais Quatre Dromadaires* (*If I Had Four Dromadaires*, 1966), Marker states: "There is life and there is its double, and photography belongs to the universe of the double. By getting close to faces you have the feeling of partaking in the life and death of human visages. This is not true: if you partake of anything at all, it is their life and death as images". Chris Marker, *Commentaires* 2: 88 (Paris: Seuil, 1967).

55      Stendhal, *La Vie de Henri Brulard*, translated by John Sturrock (London: Penguin, 1995).

56      "How to film the ladies of Bissau. Apparently the magical function of the eye was working against me there...I see her. She saw me. She knows that I see her. She drops me her glance, but just at an angle where it is still possible to act as though it was not addressed to me. And at the end the real glance straightforward, that lasted a 24th of a second, the length of a film frame."

57      The apostrophes denote Marker's own description of Yamaneko's activities.

58      In remarks made in relation to *Le Fond de l'air est rouge*, Marker commented on the contrast between the typical modes of the presentation of history in television. These images, made for rapid consumption and juxtaposed in a perpetual "haemorrhaging" stream, effectively present, Marker argues, a "history without memory": "Because they belong to television news, these images are immediately absorbed by the shifting sands on which they are founded – where illusion passes for perception – and thus disappear into the collective unconscience". Marker (1977): 10.

59    Van Cauwenberge: 235.

60    Michel de Certeau, *Heterologies: Discourse on the Other*, fifth edition (Minneapolis; London: University of Minnesota Press, 1997): 3-4.

61    See Jean Baudrillard, *Fatal Strategies*, translated by Philip Beitchman and W G J Niesluchowski, edited by Jim Fleming (New York: Semiotext[e], 1990): 186.

62    Similarly, *Le Fond de l'air est rouge*, woven together from a patchwork of unused rushes from militant films and forgotten television footage, aims to resurrect images otherwise doomed to oblivion.

63    Marker (1977): 6-7.

64    Many of Marker's recent films had only been shown at film festivals or had not received distribution. The two-part *Le Fond de l'air est Rouge* received a commissioned translation from Channel 4 Films, but, to my knowledge, was not shown in any British cinemas.

65    See, for example, Charles Ryweck, "Sans Soleil", *The Hollywood Reporter* 279: 23 (14 November 1983): 13.

66    See Derek Elley, "Sunless", *Films and Filming* August 1984: 41.

67    Steve Jenkins, "Sans Soleil", *Monthly Film Bulletin* 51: 606 (July 1984): 195.

68    Van Cauwenberge: 235. See also Terrence Rafferty, "Marker Changes Trains", *Sight and Sound* 53: 4 (autumn 1984): 284-288.

69    Chris Auty, "Sunless", *City Limits* 142 (22-28 June 1984): 30.

# Selected bibliography

**Writings on** *Sunless*

Biro, Yvette. "In the Spiral of Time", *Millennium Film Journal* (autumn/winter 1984/85): 173-177.

Perrin, Eliane. "Sunless, or the living memory of Chris. Marker", *Scope Magazine* 1 (November 1992/January 1993): 22-23.

Rafferty, Terrence. "Marker Changes Trains", *Sight and Sound* 53: 4 (autumn 1984): 284-288.

Van Cauwenberge, G D. *Chris Marker and French Documentary Filmmaking: 1962-1982* (PhD thesis, New York University, 1993).

Walsh, Michael. "Around the World, Across All Frontiers: Sans Soleil as Dépays", *CineAction!* (autumn 1989): 29-36.

**Reviews of** *Sunless*

Auty, Chris. "Sunless", *City Limits* 142 (22-28 June 1984): 30.

Conomos. "Sunless: Francophiles and the Non-Western Signifier", *Film News (Australia)* 14: 1/2 (January/February 1984): 12-13.

Eisen, Ken. "Sans Soleil", *Cinéaste* 14: 2 (1985): 44.

Elley, Derek. "Sunless", *Films and Filming* August 1984: 40-41.

Gauthier, Guy. "Sans soleil: 4001, odyssée de l'espace-temps", *La Revue du Cinéma* 380 (February 1983): 21-23.

Gerber, Jacques. *Souvenir-Ecran* (Paris: Centre Georges Pompidou, 1989) [includes excerpts from the *Sunless* press file].

Goldschmidt, Didier. "Sans soleil de Chris Marker", *Cinématographe* 87 (March 1983): 39-40.

Jeancolas, Jean-Pierre. "Sans soleil: Le monde, à la lettre", *Positif* 264 (February 1983): 3.

Jenkins, Steve. "Sans soleil (Sunless)", *Monthly Film Bulletin* 51: 606 (July 1984): 195-196.

Len. "Sans Soleil (Sunless)" *Variety* 13 April 1983: 20.

Marker, Chris. "Réécrire la mémoire: Sans soleil de Chris Marker", *Jeune Cinéma* 149 (March 1983): 25-26 [extracts from the script].

Martineau, Richard. "Sans soleil", *Séquences* 116 (April 1984): 74-75.

Rayns, Tony. [untitled], *Time Out* 722 (21-27 June 1984): 59.

Ryweck, Charles. "Sans soleil", *The Hollywood Reporter* 279: 23 (14 November 1983): 13.

"Sans soleil", *Film Français* 1931 (21 January 1983): 23.

"Sunless", *Undercut* 17 (spring 1988): 41.

"Sunless", *The Village Voice* 44 (1 November 1983): 56.

"Terminal Vertigo", *Monthly Film Bulletin* 51: 606 (July 1984): 196-197 [Marker (?) answers questions on *Sunless*].

Thirard, Paul-Louis. "Sans soleil: Ex-fans des sixties...", *Positif* 265 (March 1983): 62.

# Credits

| | |
|---|---|
| original title | Sans soleil/Sunless |
| country of production | France |
| year of production | 1982 |
| length | 99 minutes |
| gauge | 16mm |
| production company | Argos·Films |
| director | Chris. Marker |
| additional photography | Eugenio Bentivoglio, Jean-Michel Humeau, Mario Marret, Sana na N'hada, Haroun Tazieff, Danièle Tessier |
| still photographers | Martin Boschet, Roger Grange |
| special effects | Hayao Yamaneko |
| composer | Michel Krasna (electronic sounds), Mussorgsky, Sibelius |
| song | Arielle Dombasle |
| editor | Chris. Marker |

# Index

# Cinetek series

This new series encompasses important films in the history of world cinema. The series aims to be as wide-ranging as possible, and preference is given to neglected, "difficult" or confrontational films. Each book evaluates and analyses a key film, providing a detailed textual reading and a close examination of individual scenes. All books are paperback and 64 pages in length. The following titles are published or in preparation: